*The Living*
*of Re*

**By The Same Authors:**

The Joy of Reiki

# The Living Handbook of Reiki

Nalin Nirula
Renoo Nirula

MACMILLAN

First Published in India in 1958 by Whole Earth Publishing Company, P.O, Box No. 5290, New Delhi 110 021

This edition is published by Macmillan India Ltd., in 2000

MACMILLAN INDIA LIMITED

Delhi Chennai Jaipur Mumbai Patna
Bangalore Bhopal Chandigarh Coimbatore
Cuttack Guwahati Hubli Hyderabad Lucknow
Madurai Nagpur Pune Thiruvananthapuram Visakhapatnam

Companies and representatives throughout the world

ISBN 0333 93436 9

Published by Rajiv Beri for Macmillan India Limited
2/10 Ansari Road, Daryaganj, New Delhi 110002

*Cover*: The 'Hamsa' (Arabic for 'Five'), The hand of God. From a traditional Israeli good fortune motif.

*Cover Concept*: Renoo Nirula

Lasertypeset by Anvi Composers,
A-1/33 Paschim Vihar, New Delhi 110063

Printed by Rajkamal Electric Press
B-35/9, G.T. Karnal Road, Delhi 110033

*'Dedicated with love*
*to all Reiki Channels everywhere*
*for having taken a giant step in taking*
*responsibility for healing their lives*
*and choosing not to go through life*
*as helpless, hopeless victims of fate,*
*but instead, working at becoming*
*Masters of their Destiny.'*

# *Authors' Note*

# Acknowledgment

To all the Reiki Channels from whom we learnt much while teaching them; to Ranjit Sabikhi for the additional illustrations; and Harinder Singh for his assistance in producing this book.

Dr. Mikao Usui

4 February, 1801—6 January, 1887

# *Contents*

## THE SECOND BOOK

# THE FIRST BOOK

# REFLECTIONS AND REALIZATIONS

*This was written soon after Nalin Nirula received his Reiki first and second degree empowerments. These writings record and portray a significant period during the spiritual transformation of the Fourth Grandmaster of Reiki. These were the first of his writings coming directly from touching higher realities.*

From the age of nine I have travelled my own path internally, and sometimes, externally. Many things came to me while I was grossly ignorant of much. And thirty-five years later I find that while much has happened, much is the same. And yet there is radical change.

What were glimpses of mysticism in yesteryears are realizations of today. The hints of a life other than that experienced externally are inner realities now. Having travelled far afield has brought me closer to something within.

With this experience came the realization that our inner universe manifests outwardly as well. Be this in health or disease; be it in joy and happiness or negativity. If we want change externally, it must first take place within us. Otherwise it is only a mechanical patch-up job. The external repair is also needed, but more than that is the need for radical inner change.

The change comes only from the desire for change for we really do not know what we have to do for it. If we knew already, we would have done it. From this desire and its reflection in life's mirror we find our way.

The external situation gives us incentives to move on towards higher consciousness. The incentives are uncomfortable and necessarily so, because if we are comfortable and happy, what is the incentive to move on?

Internal discontent is to be nurtured carefully. It is the fire in the engine that will drive us onward. A friend recently asked me from within his heart, almost despairingly, 'When will this relentless pursuit end?' That moved me and crystallized an understanding.

Let it not end. Be relentless.

You will find your own path just as I found mine. If you want to change it, you can—by changing your inner world, giving up negativities. My reflections and realizations may not be yours, which is perfectly alright. Some of these may find resonance with yours, which is also fine.

These writings help clarify my own perceptions and are an inner cleansing for me. They arise from direct experience and do not require validation from anyone. Your realizations do not require validation either, for life's mirror of your inner situation will guide you. On your path through life you will experience some hint, some superior vibration that will move you away from the dullness of negative emotions.

Somewhere and sometime you will find a fleeting musk-fragrance of pure love. You will follow it, and after much searching realize that it actually came from within.

Another who has this, will perhaps cross your way, and in his presence your dormant joyous self will resonate in harmony. Or it will come unasked and unknown and steal silently away.

You will be left experiencing a deep healing of the spirit, and regret at its passing. That healing resonance is love. And if we share that same inner universe of joy and love and of being healed, it will manifest around you in your life and the life of those you touch. Each one of us has that potency.

When many do this, the whole external universe must change. The greater the disorder, the greater the urgent need for healing.

Love is infectious—get it and pass it around.

It is the highest healing.

# LOVE

If I don't love myself then I can't love my family, my neighbour, or anyone else. If I really hate and dislike myself, my life, then I shall equally hate and dislike others and their lives and even that they live.

*If I don't have something, I can't give it to you—I can only give what I have.*

When love is blocked, I can't love artificially—it makes me ill at ease to the point of physical disease.

So first, I must find and connect with that unconditional loving, healing energy, through the grace of a Master who is himself so connected.

Such a Master is able to reveal my original wholeness. When I have that, only then am I able to pass it on.

No other is required to confirm your experiencing of this loving healing energy.

Ask yourself seriously, 'Am I willing to be responsible for being whole and complete? Do I want it?'

And then all you need to do is to get connected in an attitude of thankfulness, and experience the flow of love within, which will then appear externally as well.

You will yourself directly experience being whole, complete and healed. Others around you will be touched by the overflow.

# PAIN

Pain is terribly distorting to our consciousness and mind. When we are in mental, emotional or bodily pain and dullness we may not be able to understand our true purpose in life.

But at the same time, sufficient experience of pain drives us to look for non-mechanical solutions, a healing, and we may come across some spiritualists by whose causeless mercy we can get relief. If we are open to this receiving, then we can immediately transcend our inner pain.

We can do this by being connected to a pure source of healing spiritual energy through one who himself is so connected. Then, even though we may have many defects, our contact with pure spiritual nature begins to overcome all contaminations. In time this manifests in ourselves to a greater and greater degree, just as an iron rod placed in the fire gradually takes on the qualities of the original, itself becoming fire and light.

Spiritual re-connection re-establishes a free flow of joy within us which overrides all constraints of matter and material existence. Pain is the blocking of the flow of joy at the heart—and this is our fundamental disease, regardless of the variety of forms in which disease results may appear and the masks they may wear.

The experience of joy is of value beyond measure. It is available to all who want it and all who are open. It purifies the heart and resides there, and even casual contact with such a one whose heart is pure is immensely healing.

# OFFENSE

In spiritual life, in the quest for becoming whole and complete in self-development, *'aparadh'*—offense, criticism—against the spiritually advanced persons is considered particularly dangerous. Those who willfully and obstinately commit *aparadh* due to arrogance and false self-importance suffer severe blocking reactions in body and mind.

Their spiritual advancement is retarded. External suffering intensifies. This is a reflection of the inner suffering and pain felt due to an offense not resolved. Criticism, envy, hatred for anyone blocks us internally, and when directed against the spiritually advanced, the reaction is much more intense.

Awareness of suffering destroys false ego. And when even this fails, a lower level of consciousness is granted—appropriate for the inner attitudes in this very lifetime.

This lower consciousness prevents the same type of *aparadh* from having further reaction to some extent, but the lack of awareness is not desirable at all because the tendency to commit offense remains and reactions must follow.

A dog may habitually cross the street disregarding traffic signals and it won't be prosecuted, but eventually the dog will be run over by a vehicle and be killed. Similarly we can choose to be either god-ly or dog-ly internally, and the inner reality will manifest outwardly in this very lifetime's experience of consciousness.

Only by pursuing spiritual wholeness can we defeat this victimization. The biggest obstacle is the tendency of the mind to criticize freely. The function of the mind is to evaluate, choose one over another—to judge and criticize.

When this happens in the field of emotion or evaluation of spirituality, the mind is totally incompetent because it functions only in the area of material knowledge—the known past.

The conditioned mind cannot enter the area of direct perception, direct experience, and when it tries to do that there is severe mental indigestion.

The mind is quite helpless.

If we don't deal with this by protecting and cleansing the mind and heart, our inherent spiritual nature will rectify it for us through hard cleansing reactions for our benefit, so that love may flow again.

This is the genesis and end-purpose of suffering.

So we understand that *aparadh* is detrimental to spiritual advancement, and lack of spiritual advancement destroys all kinds of happiness in this life, here and now.

# 'LETTING GO'

That which has been accumulated must move dynamically or it must otherwise decay, causing us discomfort. Even material wealth decays unless put to work, unless it circulates and is generating something or serving a purpose.

Internally this happens when we hold onto past emotional memories. Holding onto the past interferes with my present and I am naturally miserable.

'But when I let go of what I have, don't I lose something that is valuable to me? So why should I do it?' Ask yourself what is so valuable about something that makes you ill mentally, emotionally and physically. Does it have a value so that you can gain some attention, sympathy, affection from those around you? Is it important to you so that you can manipulate others? Is it from fear?

If it is, then ask whether the cost is worthwhile. Because you are paying for it by being so ill at ease, and that is *dis-ease.*

Only ask this and wait with honest expectation and you will get the true reply from the heart—don't reject it. Don't let your old mental image of yourself interfere with the answer. If the answer is painful just stay with it, understand it. There is no right or wrong about this—do not judge yourself please. Pain tells you something.

If you understand in a child-like way keeping no filters between you and the answer from within, you will go beyond your present state and experience a major healing.

So, experience 'letting go' without judging. It is very healing. It rids you of rotten garbage—whatever form it may be in. It is most cleansing.

You say you do not have any belief in the experience of this? That this is 'impractical theory'?

No, it is not theory. You have already experienced this many times, especially when it affected your body, and after 'letting go' you were better emotionally and physically.

'When was this?' you ask.

This was when you had an unnatural tightness in your gut, your body was physically constipated—and then one day you let go emotionally and experienced all-round relief—that was it.

Now consciously let go mentally and emotionally. Drop the old inner garbage and experience a major healing.

# RELIGIOSITY, SPIRITUALITY, FALSE EGO AND DISEASE

Religion means a 'search for the Truth', and religiosity is the practise of method, rules and regulations in pursuit of that goal. The goal itself is attaining to the 'highest truth'—which is the spiritual, the Divine or God.

The highest form of religiosity cleanses our false ego. At the same time it does not eliminate all negativities from us. *Ahankaar,* or false ego born of pride reflects the inner attitude of having something which the other does not. It comes from the attitude of possessing something exclusive while the other is deprived of it. There is a sense of superiority in this.

*Ahankaar* diminishes us by putting a knot in our hearts, choking the flow of love, and we experience inner pain. Cut off from this vital nourishment, unable to digest negativities nor eliminate them, breeds within us anger, envy, hatred, frustration, despair and hopelessness. When this emotional-mental discomfort becomes hard reality, it is *dis*-ease, and eventually, 'disease'. Mechanically treating these external reflections alone is of limited value. Perhaps a different methodology is needed.

Religiosity at its best smashes gross false ego, our attachments to false images born of pride. It rectifies these attitudes while soothing our inner pain. Is there any loss in this for one who follows religiously and ritually the principles of non-sinful, regulated life?

Strictly speaking such a one is a law-abiding citizen in the quest for spirituality—no meat eating, no intoxication, no gambling, no sex life outside of marriage (and then only for the purpose of procreation.)

The practitioner gets help in his efforts by being connected with spiritual energies through his *guru*. The very act of approaching and surrendering to the *guru* is in itself cleansing-purifying. As a consequence the *sadhaka* (practitioner) develops a higher taste, a satisfaction in avoiding the lower urges of nature which limit his thinking and activities. Instead he practises religiosity in the expectation that he will be healed totally. But, in the process of his *sadhana,* practise, he does not realize that it is only a *sadhan*—a means to get him ready for the actual experience of spirituality. It is not empowered for the final step of being fully linked to the divine and therefore it is not radically effective for changing one's life. The final goal is not achieved.

In this hard practise of following rules and regulations he develops the opposite of gross material false ego. He develops a most subtle *sattvic* false ego—a false ego in the mode of material goodness, as it were. A sense of superiority arising from following the form of being humble, or being known as humble—an advanced spiritualist. A *Brahmin*—establishing himself in the spirit or *Brahma*, being the exclusive devotee of the Lord, the Divine. 'Exclusive' also as in excluding others who are not devotees, who are mere sense-gratifying *karmis*.

Of all false egos, this subtle false ego in the mode of goodness is the most poisonous because it is the most difficult to detect, and where the false ego is so nourished, the spiritual self does not manifest fully.

Such a spiritualist may lose many things in his life—his family, his health, his wealth. This is a rigorous and accelerated purification. He experiences pain at his losses but the religious connection and faith already established take care of him somehow. When he experiences his losses being equivalent to final death, and physically he may come to this point as well, a different situation presents itself. If he has followed a genuine line of spiritualism and hasn't given up, then a quantum shift in consciousness takes place when he is empty of everything.

If he is ready at the moment of this ego-death, when the mind is perfectly silenced, the Divine directly intervenes giving him the highest spiritually nourishing connection which knows no rules and regulations.

It is boldly outside the jurisdiction of *sadhana.* It occurs instantly in the absence of material cause. Then causeless love manifests within the heart spontaneously, and one only has to distribute it wherever it so demands.

Where the religious teachings followed have a genuine foundation, then even with his remaining defects, *sattvic* false ego and all, he who is devoted to this work is never vanquished in this world or the next.

But the followers of ritual religiosity, bound-up by codes and 'law' may not see this, and not seeing, they may reject the truly enlightened spiritualist judging him as fallen.

This would be to their great and terrible detriment.

# UNCONDITIONAL LOVE

Cut short all process of connecting with love. Ask boldly and deeply, 'If unconditional love is without conditions, why must there be this or that pre-condition for it to come to me?'

Do this and you will immediately find the next higher step. You only have to inquire from the heart—shout out with courage, without artifice and without intellectualization.

Drop all *concepts* of what is the highest. Ask, demand, insist on being satisfied only by the highest realization—whatever that may be. Be open and ready to receive it.

Grace will flow and you will directly experience the next beautiful flowering of your true nature. It cannot be denied.

# DISPUTES, HARMONY AND DISHARMONY

*'Once we are Reiki channels does it mean we can't have disputes, nor need to defend ourselves, our property, our "rights" (whatever they may be)?'*

This is not a silly theoretical question. We have had people challenge Reiki channels, the worth of Reiki and their healing activities on this basis. And, in fact, we find Reiki channels involved in disputes, court cases, in very sticky situations from time to time. So what does this mean?

Does this mean, as is implied or even openly stated by challengers—that the Reiki channels who resort to the process of law as administered by society are in some way reduced, or does it somehow suddenly prove that Reiki is not a 'superior' energy and the Reiki channels working with Reiki and so involved are therefore 'fallen' in some way? Or is Reiki a failure?

Not at all.

Reiki is a *harmonizing* energy whether the activity is positive or negative, so-called 'good' or 'bad'. It is an erroneous assumption that all Reiki channels should suddenly lie down, roll over and give up all appropriate, lawful means for the protection, conservation of their life and property. This is the envious concept of a person who does not have any Reiki experience, and feels the inner need to challenge the good fortune of those who have, little realizing they can also have this for the asking!

Their argument is: 'You are supposed to be "spiritual", therefore, you should not use the legal process. Reiki, God or the divine should directly intervene, and if they do not, then you fail, Reiki fails!'

Such misleading arguments reflect the great need such persons have for healing—it is almost like a child's temper tantrum. Send them healing with the request that they too receive Reiki love and light to revive their shrivelled hearts!

Where there is a dispute, an argument, a fight between persons, Reiki healing can and does harmonize the situation.

It is not that with Reiki disputes will not take place, sometimes they will due to present karma or old karma—it does not matter which; but most importantly, the disharmony will settle in the best possible way provided Reiki is flowing sufficiently and there is desire for harmony. And throughout this, the interests of Reiki channels are specially protected. That is the experience of Reiki channels.

Reiki channels may outwardly be living their lives like ordinary persons, disputes and all, but there is a great difference between their inner state and what is driving them, what is behind them. . . And that is Reiki, the supreme harmonist and protector.

## Divine Reiki Lineage

*The Supreme Spiritual Person–Source of all sources, Source of Reiki*

Mikao Usui *(O Sensei–GRANDMASTER AND FOUNDER)*

Chujiro Hayashi *(2ND GRANDMASTER)*

Hawayo Hiromi Takata *(3RD GRANDMASTER)*

Phyllis Lee Furomoto

David Jarrell - Rohini Desai - Sandeep Chakot

Harjit Lamba

Nalin Nirula *(7TH SENSEI AND 4TH GRANDMASTER)*

Renoo Nirula *(8TH SENSEI)*

# REIKI LINEAGE NOTES

Initiating Masters and Instructing Masters are always considered as being equal, but in practise, the Instructing Master (*shiksha-guru*) has a greater influence and role in the development of the individual. (This is confirmed in practise where the Reiki Mastership final attunements are by *knowledge alone* and this enhances and multiplies the new Master's healing capacity manifold.)

Traditional spiritual lineages acknowledge this by simultaneously tracing lineages equally through the *shiksha* line as well as the *diksha* (initiation) line. Often, where a *diksha* line is not a prominent contributor, it may be dropped altogether.

After receiving her Master's empowerment from Rohini Desai, Harjit Lamba met with David Jarrell in a special meeting where he conveyed authentic knowledge of Reiki to her. Sandeep Chakot conveyed the Reiki First and Second Degrees to Nalin Nirula, while Harjit Lamba conveyed the Master's empowerment to him.

The Fourth Grandmaster internally meditated on and worked with higher Reiki procedures for about six months after receiving his Mastership. During this process he received complete and authentic higher and mystic knowledge directly from the previous Grandmasters of Reiki, and Reiki Herself.

*The Masters created by him have also been given these complete re-discovered attunement (initiation) techniques and knowledge as used by him for Reiki initiation.* At any one time, there is only one Grandmaster available on the planet.

**21 Independent Reiki Masters and Teachers of Traditional Reiki Created by the Fourth Grandmaster of Reiki**

Renoo Nirula
Rajni Anhal (UK)
Peeyush Andlay
Meher Charna
Kavita Chawla
Charmaine Malik
Asha Sabikhi
Vijay Bansal
Ritu Uttam
Nita Gupta Jain
Protima Gupta
Guy Alter (Israel)
Nira Tyler (Australia)
Ulrich Petsch (Germany/South Africa)
Nicola Petsch (UK/South Africa)
Aruna Jain
Ariel Goldman (Israel)
Batya Goldman (Israel)
Ronit Tamir (Israel)
Daniel Avgi (Israel)
Daphne Zepos (France/Greece)

*(Listing complete upto June 1998)*

# REIKI LINEAGE

Although Reiki is the same everywhere, the level you are connected to depends on your present internal spiritual development (vibratory rate) and the level where the Master is himself connected—a Master cannot give you more than what is his connecting capacity, just as you cannot spend more than what is in your pocket.

Each of us gets our Reiki connection according to our karmic situation. By working on ourselves further (which is also karma) we can maximize our self-healing, wherever our starting level with Reiki may be. *There is never any loss with Reiki no matter where you start!*

'Grandmaster' *(O Sensei)* indicates a Reiki Master through whom authentic, higher confidential knowledge of Reiki is revealed and passed on, and one who does not contradict or violate the teachings of previous Grandmasters. Such a one is considered to be a 'Master of Masters'—one who can heal and advance even the Masters.

The appearance of a Grandmaster is rare. Before leaving her body, and as recorded by her students (see the writings of Fran Brown), Master Takata declared that of her created Masters none would be Grandmaster, and did not see it fit to reveal the complete knowledge to any of her created Masters. Each Master received procedures that were somewhat different from that of another Master, in accordance with Third Grandmaster Takata's empowered vision.

In 1994, two American Reiki Masters in the line of Grandmaster Hawayo Takata forecast the appearance of the Fourth Grandmaster of Reiki. They broadcast a message in the cosmos through Reiki that an appropriate Reiki Master from India should contact them. When this event took place, they conveyed a special two-part request to the Reiki Master who visited with them.

The American Reiki Masters were concerned that much unauthentic information and procedures about Reiki were prevalent in the system as practised in India and many parts of the world.

So they gave the Indian Master the basic attunement knowledge and the authentic mystic symbols of Reiki, which were quite different from what has been given in many parts of the world, including India and the United States. This incomplete knowledge was creating a barrier to the growth of Reiki channels. Due to this the Reiki energy channelled by them was and is only about 25 per cent to 30 per cent of the maximum potential achieveable as compared to when using the authentic symbols and procedures. The second part of the request was more unusual:

> When you return to India, a Master from Delhi will contact you asking for the Mastership . . . When he does, asking for the Mastership, please give it to him without hesitation or delay, for he is already a Master by qualification and only needs the final knowledge and Master's attunement . . . and through him authentic Reiki will spread throughout the world.

In 1995, Nalin Nirula was that Reiki channel who received this Master's initiation without delay from the seventh Reiki Master contacted. (The other six having indicated that receiving Master's initiation would take a few years.)

By the middle of 1996, thanks to the grace of Reiki and the previous Grandmasters, *O Sensei* Nalin Nirula had rediscovered the complete and original attunement knowledge and methods of the previous Grandmasters working independently of any living Master.

This was a difficult time for Nalin as he had to rely deeply on the inner mystic guidance he was receiving. Later, the lower mind would question and create doubts. During this time he was only able to receive clairvoyant guidance from Renoo Nirula as to the final results of whatever procedures he was doing during the attunements, which confirmed he was on the right path. This was because at that time Renoo Nirula was not a Master and was therefore unable to look behind the mystic shields protecting the confidentiality of the sacred attunement processes. Furthermore, he could not discuss any of the procedures with her as he was under oath not to disclose the advanced knowledge for six months.

The final confirmation came from the end-results where group after group of Reiki channels reached higher and higher levels of spiritual awakening and healing capacity each time the next procedure or refinement was re-discovered and applied during the attunements.

In June 1996, Renoo Nirula received her Mastership from Nalin Nirula, and at that time, her clairvoyant vision was permitted to penetrate the mystic shields that protect the sacred attunement process.

With her special clairvoyant capacity she re-confirmed the development of the Fourth Grandmaster's attunement process as completely authentic, it being channelled to him directly by Dr Mikao Usui. Based on her connecting with the previous Grandmasters, she suggested certain valuable refinements in the procedures which the Fourth Grandmaster has incorporated in the attunement process.

The Fourth Grandmaster considers the creation of Reiki Masters as a joint collaboration between him and *Sensei*

Renoo Nirula with the blessings of the Divine and the previous Grandmasters. All their created Masters receive the same complete Reiki knowledge and procedures as they themselves use.

At this time Grandmaster Nirula empowers advanced Reiki channels and Masters of Reiki further, also through Mystic Keys revealed to him from the confidential Lotus Sutra verses as first discovered by Founder-Grandmaster Dr Mikao Usui. This empowerment and guidance has thus far been unavailable to current Masters of Reiki, although the Grandmasters were fully aware of this knowledge.

This empowerment ('Reiki-3 Plus' or '3+') is second in potency to the Master's empowerment. It is of particular benefit for the Reiki degree known as Reiki-3A, because it provides a healing capacity that works like the Master Symbol for healing others.

The Master Symbol received by Reiki-3A is meant only for their own healing because its purpose is to *attune others* to Reiki and to *increase* one's own divine enlightenment. Used freely for the healing of others (as by many Reiki Masters) is the cause of the Reiki Masters receiving severe health and life situation reactions. Here the burden of karmic exchange is more than what they can digest or transform especially if they are not perfectly transparent. False ego causes absorption of karmic reaction—this is being 'not perfectly transparent' where we introduce our own 'coloured' personal ego-based bias.

This special Lotus Sutra empowerment is available only through Grandmaster Nalin Nirula and *Sensei* Renoo Nirula.

*No other Masters have been authorized by them at this time to convey this particular empowerment further.*

# FOREWORD
## by the Fourth Grandmaster of Reiki

Greetings, love, light and joy to all Reiki channels everywhere.

Ever since we connected with Reiki, we have been regularly approached by channels who are uncertain as to how Reiki is to be applied in their daily life once they have their initiation and connection with Reiki.

We understand that to be connected with Reiki and to heal ourself of all material 'disease' is the highest purpose of life. This is made possible only by the unconditional grace of the Divine through the agency of a Master. If, after having received such a precious jewel, you are unable to move forward adequately due to lack of further guidance or information, this empowered and empowering book of knowledge is meant for you.

Reiki descends from the highest spiritual levels in a spiritual lineage and in all such lineages two distinct lines are traceable. The ancient *Vedas* (books of knowledge) classify these as the *diksha* (initiation empowerment) line, and *shiksha* (knowledge and guidance empowerment) line of the *guru* or Master.

Traditionally, the *diksha* and *shiksha gurus* (Masters) are the same person. However, formally they may be different, and as far as instruction is concerned, there is no limit to how many Masters one may take instruction from.

It is perfectly understandable that if one has received a particular level of guidance and requires more advanced guidance, then one may have to approach another Master. And here, if the knowledge given is authentic, there is only gain. Sometimes the Master will require the individual to be re-initiated especially where the previous initiations did not take effect (refer to our book, *The Joy of Reiki*, for more details). Knowledge and guidance which dissolve the bindings of karma—such as the knowledge contained in this book—may be conveyed only by a Master who is so empowered.

This is because only such a Master is able to convey authoritative guidance which is effective. At the same time, no karmic entanglements come to him for liberating others from their karmic burdens. We point this out in case you, in your understandable enthusiasm to share this knowledge with others, begin to instruct them from the position of a Master without having the empowerment and safety backup systems of authorized Masters.

If someone is interested in knowing more, let him study this book himself, or he may approach a self-realized Master directly.

Those who have Reiki-2 and Reiki-3 initiations will also benefit from this *Living Handbook of Reiki* because the fundamentals given here are the foundation for the advanced degree methods of healing. Those with advanced degrees may use all of these methods with the *additional* usage of the mystic empowerment symbols given to them.

Discussing matters contained in this book with non-Reiki channels is not advisable as they will not have a self-experienced understanding of these matters and *their theoretical or speculative views may impede and disturb your progress.* Similarly, discussing these matters with Reiki channels who have no knowledge of our teachings *may generally be avoided.*

The most authentic way to approach these teachings is to *live them in your daily life and find out for yourself what is most appealing to you and most appropriate for you.* All the methods described work; but some methods may appeal more and others not—which is perfectly fine. However, we suggest that you work with all the techniques so as to understand their potential, as all methods given are freely workable.

*Everything in this* Living Handbook *is fully authentic, empowered and alive with Reiki.* If you accept the knowledge here with that appreciation, with thankfulness and in surrender to Reiki, you will receive all the necessary guidance you need from this beautiful *Living Handbook of Reiki.* If you desire additional confirmation, internally request Reiki for it, and that too shall appear.

If you live life with an awareness of the principles of Reiki, being aware of your true higher self, and being in an attitude of gratitude and surrender to Reiki, your life will be full of joy and abundance. This is the promise of Reiki to all who accept responsibility for healing their lives, who take this first major step towards becoming Masters of their Destiny.

Our understanding and teaching of Reiki-1 is that, *Reiki-1 is in no way to be considered 'lesser' than Reiki-2 or the higher degrees.* There is only a difference in the quantum and capability of energy available, *not the quality.*

Please understand that *all* Reiki levels are *perfect.* Reiki-1 is very perfect, Reiki-2 is highly perfect, and Reiki-3 and beyond are most perfect! *Never make the blunder of thinking of Reiki-1 as 'less'.*

Reiki-1 and Reiki-2 degrees empower you to create abundance in your life in all areas. Reiki-3 is meant for furthering the inner detachment from all material issues which starts manifesting with advancement in Reiki healing.

Traditionally Reiki-3 was meant for Masters only. Today the energy of Reiki-3 is also available as the Reiki-3A degree (without the Master's knowledge of attunements) so that one may progress further spiritually without taking on the commitment of the Master. One may consider this step on reaching maturity in Reiki and in one's life situation. It is not necessary for most Reiki channels.

We teach in practical form that everything achievable with Reiki-2 is achievable with Reiki-1, and those same teachings are given here. All the information we present in our *Reiki Experience™ Seminars* is reproduced here in a concise form, including information that has thus far been maintained as confidential, especially knowledge of (i) how to send healing across space and time; (ii) how to dissolve karmic blocks in the body of the healee or obstacles in the way of healing/creating situations; (iii) 'instant healing'; (iv) psychic protection.

This facility has generally been available only through Reiki-2 methodology until now. This is the first time that fully authentic knowledge of this capability at the Reiki-1 level is being revealed by us for the benefit of all Reiki channels worldwide.

Although this book is technically oriented out of necessity, *ultimately there is no technique for Reiki.* Healing is a spontaneous outpouring of loving energy activated by our intention and desire, and the mere presence of a purified Reiki channel is sufficient to heal, to harmonize in a radical way.

As we may not always be on that spontaneous platform, we may not *be* so purified, and we may not always *be living* in an attitude of gratitude—so for those times, *technique will convey sufficient healing without fail.*

The origin and refinement of many techniques of healing here are due greatly to *Sensei* Renoo Nirula who clairvoyantly observed how spontaneous healing took place in our presence. Many of the techniques were received from our first Reiki Master. The healing techniques given have been refined from a combination of such knowledge, observation, higher guidance, revelations and verified end-results. *Sensei* Renoo's desire to elevate all Reiki channels everywhere to a level of non-helplessness has actually resulted in the appearance of this book.

Incorporated as part of the teachings are meditations and other measures which are not the Reiki experience directly, but are very helpful at the energy body level and enhance the Reiki experience.

We present all this information as we see it and receive it also through meditation and clairvoyant vision as statements of observed fact not requiring detailed discussion or explanation.

We have been informed by research scholars and spiritualists that our expositions on these matters are in concordance with previous authentic Vedic spiritual authorities and the authorities of advanced mystic traditions elsewhere in the world, although we have no great detailed book of knowledge of these traditions, and do not claim to be Vedic scholars.

While our book *The Joy of Reiki* may also be studied alongside for additional insights, this *Handbook* is self-contained and stands by itself as a complete practical guide for the Reiki practitioner as well as the Reiki Master.

Finally, please remember, *Reiki always works*, but our perceptions and understanding of Reiki may be incomplete and therefore sometimes we may be tempted to think that Reiki doesn't quite work. When this happens, look within and correct whatever needs correction, without guilt, without self-blame.

If you have witnessed or experienced 'miraculous' healings by Reiki channels, you should know that a lot of preparatory work was done by them in different ways before they reached where they did. By sincerely following the teachings given here, you too can master the techniques of effortless healing.

By presenting this information and by your acceptance of it, we are in the position of the Master who empowers by knowledge, effectively removing the shackles of ignorance and karma.

And even though we may never meet in bodily form, our vibrations have already met across time and space, and Reiki has already reached out to touch you and heal you through these empowered instruments: this book and our healing desire, *reaching all who touch this book or read it or hear from it.*

As you accept this with thanks and gratitude to Reiki, so shall the knowledge be revealed to you further from this *Living Handbook of Reiki*. That is the only qualification required for progressing after having received your Reiki initiation.

*I, Nalin Nirula, fully empowered Seventh Sensei (Initiating Master and Teacher) and Fourth Grandmaster of Reiki in the line of Mikao Usui (O Sensei), on this day do hereby empower with all highest Mystic Potencies the knowledge contained herein for the qualified ones for whom it is meant.*

*Given under the hand and seal of NALIN NIRULA, Seventh Sensei and Fourth Grandmaster of Reiki, on this most blessed day of Ramanavami, the tenth day of October, in the year one thousand nine hundred and ninety seven, at A-14, Anand Niketan, New Delhi, India.*

NALIN NIRULA
*4th Grandmaster*

## *Quotations from the 4th Grandmaster*

'With Reiki there are no more "O" for "Obstacles" or "O, what should I do?" All the Os are for "Opportunities to heal". Whenever you are feeling helpless, immediately send healing to the situation—helplessness will vanish instantly, and you will experience a free flow of joy in your heart centre.'

* * *

'Seeming miracles can take place in healing, and when they do you must understand that it is the unconditional grace of the divine.... the results are never in our hands—only the divine healing energy. We are not the "doers". This understanding develops a proper detachment in the healing work. When the results do not appear as expected, we must look at what we are doing and see if we have overlooked something. Request guidance from Reiki and you will soon come to know what to rectify. This is *commitment* to results while being *detached* from results.'

* * *

# ACCESSING AND ACCEPTING THE TEACHINGS

*Renoo Nirula*

The *Living Handbook of Reiki* contains the active teachings of Reiki and through its pages and the written word flow divine healing energies. In order to receive the highest benefits of the teachings, the *Living Handbook* is to be treated with respect. In practical terms it means, for example, not leaving it lying around casually, nor keeping it on the floor nor in an unclean place.

When you first receive the *Living Handbook* and before you begin your formal study of it, it is useful to raise the book to your third eye wisdom *chakra* (the area between the eyebrows), and respectfully (mentally) accept receiving the highest benefits from the *Living Handbook*, and then place it briefly at the heart centre—the resting place of Reiki.

It may be useful to first read the whole book, then carefully study the teachings given, taking your time to absorb each topic fully.

The *Living Handbook is self-revealing*. This means, as your level of understanding or expertise in healing increases, the book will reveal new insights through these same pages. Respect for the book and its teachings, and being in an attitude of gratitude will give you the highest benefits.

> At the end of the *Living Handbook* there is a section which is *sealed*. It contains advanced knowledge. *Do not open* this until you have worked sufficiently with the information and material given in the rest of the book for at least seven consecutive days.

## 21-DAY JOURNAL NOTES

Name: Date:

Briefly list below the ailments you are suffering from at this time and any old ailments you had suffered from including surgeries, accidents.

Sometimes, 'old ailments' reappear for a while in some form. These are old links in the chain of disease that also need healing (which is why they have surfaced). Often, we hear people say, 'I thought *that* problem was finished with, but now it seems to have come up again.'

In this private journal, briefly record the progress of your condition during the first 21 days of Reiki-healing after studying this book, looking at all areas: physical, mental, emotional.

This is important as it will help you to keep track of your health and abundance gains, especially at the times when you may not be certain that the quality of your life has changed for the better.

# 21-DAY JOURNAL NOTES

## First Seven Days

## 21-DAY JOURNAL NOTES

Second Seven Days

# 21-DAY JOURNAL NOTES

## Third Seven Days

# PRACTISE OF REIKI

- You are not expected to become an 'instant' expert on everything that has been given in this book. Take your time to absorb the information and its practical applications.
- Everything that has been given to you is fully authentic, arising purely out of practical experience and realization, tested through Reiki clairvoyance and verified by end-results. *Nothing given here is speculative or theory!*
- This book contains everything you need to know, and if you are in doubt, request Reiki to guide you, and you will receive clarification internally, or from this book itself, or an external source.
- During the first 21-day healing-cleansing cycle a massive input of energy is given to you through the agency of the *Sensei,* far in excess of your present channelling capacity.

Its purpose is to boost your self-healing radically and rapidly. This extra energy is with you for 21 days. During this time if you sincerely do touch-body self-healing at every one of the 26 positions (31 points) as taught, at the end of 21 days there will be a major shift in your inner and external health *and* life situation.

You may continue this daily healing after 21 days as well for maximum benefit. From time to time you may do touch-body healing only at major chakras and knees and at specific trouble spots *('Partial Point Reiki')*. However, *the more healing you do at every specified point, the greater the healing result.*

At any time that you wish to maximize healing, go through a 21-day full self-healing programme.

- **The most important daily practices are:**

  **Full touch-body Reiki** (1½ hours or more for adults; 15-40 minutes for children/teenagers), daily during the 21-day cycles, less if partial point Reiki is being done. Remember, you can do the full body touch Reiki over two or three or more sessions during the day, starting from where you left off previously.

  Typical Daily Schedule for Self-healing (Quick Method):

  1. On waking up in the morning, close the Attitude of Gratitude.
  2. Immediately open the Attitude of Gratitude.
  3. Do a quick healing of the 31 points sequentially once in 24 hours—say 1 minute each. This establishes the efficient sequential Reiki flow.
  4. Subsequently, do the points again in any convenient order according to time and situation.
  5. In this way you can do Reiki 24 hours a day without being stressed for time.
  6. Remember, Reiki healing does not require any 'concentration' or meditation from you—you may be doing Reiki while watching TV, socializing, etc.

  **'Partial Point Reiki'** is when you are able only to do the main chakras and a few select points daily. For a few days this may be alright, but over a longer period of time this leads to a diminishing of your Reiki-generated good fortune. This is generally not a good idea as you will start experiencing some decrease in the positive growth and fortune and will have to work harder at healing yourself to overcome this. *There are no shortcuts to Reiki results.*

  **Cleansing Meditations** (1 to 5 minutes each = 3 to 15 minutes per day), minimum once a day *(Appendix-1)*.

  **Protection Shield** whenever leaving the home (or even having it at home if the home environment is currently very negative).

  **Cleansing** of the home and work environment. *(Appendix 3)*.

# THE SECOND BOOK

# 1

# Introduction

The first few pages following give a simplified and summarized overview of the basic teachings. Here, final conclusions are stated, the explanations and reasons for which are dealt with progressively through the rest of the *Living Handbook*. The topics covered follow a specific order.

The reasons for this format are: In our *Joy of Reiki*™ *Seminars,* after exploring fundamentals, conclusions are arrived at and some of these are stated as a helpful summary in the beginning of our *Seminar Reference Manual.* The material covered here usually follows the order as is given in our seminar manual.

We have retained this format as we intend that the *Living Handbook* be used everywhere by Reiki Masters as just such a teaching manual and a study guide. We envisage that those who will be accessing the *Living Handbook* would already have sufficient background of Reiki and would have attended a Reiki Seminar where at least some of these topics would have been discussed and explored.

The last appendix of the *Living Handbook* gives a suggested format for a two-day Reiki-1 Seminar based on our experience of teaching Reiki worldwide in different cultural environments cutting across the whole socioeconomic spectrum.

The format may be simplified further according to the level of the initiates' receptivity—for example, children between 8 and 14 years of age do not need a seminar lasting more than a few hours—a day at the most. Examples of both, 'Simple' and 'Full Format' seminars are given in the appendix to the sealed section.

Detailed 'high fundamental' explanations are not required for simple folk, and trying to impress them with 'knowledge' is counter-productive. The minimum information that a person needs is sufficient—*Reiki is not so much a matter of knowledge as much as a matter of 'experiencing and doing'*.

The information given in the *Living Handbook* is meant for Reiki channels of different capacities, having varying degrees of interest in the healing technicalities.

Information in the following section, 'Meaning and Features of Reiki', may be shared with others as needed—the key understanding being: 'Reiki healing makes any disease or trauma condition better, regardless of philosophy, religion, faith or belief or the therapies being currently used.'

Avoid getting caught up in useless argument!

# 2

# *Meaning and Features of Reiki*

## Meaning

- REIKI (pronounced *'Ray-key'*) is a Japanese word
- *Rei* ('*ray*')—Universal
- *Ki ('key')*—Life Force Energy = *Spirit*

## Features

- Reiki is a natural, spiritual healing modality (not limited by material considerations), and which is totally *independent of religion, belief and faith systems.* Reiki is freely available from the universe.
- *Reiki healing empowerment is only receiveable through attunement/initiation by a Master of Reiki who is himself connected to Reiki through the initiation process.*
- The first priority is to heal oneself.
- Reiki is *taken* up by the healee and not 'given' by the Reiki channel. We are Reiki channels making Reiki *available. We are not the real healers,* although for convenience we may term ourselves as healers.
- The energy flow comes from the spiritual source via the *antahkaran* ('pillar of light', or the pathway connecting to the 'final eternal cause' or spiritual

source) entering through the Crown chakra, going past the Third eye chakra, past the Throat chakra, collecting at the Heart chakra and from there flowing to the hands, and then further to the body wherever the hands are placed.

- **Reiki acts to harmonize** at the energy body (aura) level, physical body level, emotional body level, mental body level and is therefore a holistic or whole and complete system of healing. Reiki flows directly to the chakras and from there to the endocrine system that produces hormones. The hormonal system and genetic (karmic) programming of our body directs the functioning of the organs and systems in our body, and thus the balance of health.

- **Reiki channels are not doctors** (although a number of doctors today are becoming Reiki channels)—*never interfere with nor discourage* healee's ongoing therapy. As the healee's health improves and positive results appear, the doctors would adjust therapies accordingly. The healee should convey to the doctor that he is undergoing Reiki healing.

- **Do not be attached to results.** The healee automatically draws as much energy as is required and appropriate at the time, governed by internal higher intelligence. Reiki channels only *make available* the healing energy. Do not pass judgement on the healee for his condition in life or what he may be suffering from, as from a 'superior' or judgemental platform.

- Always encourage the healee in his search for regaining health, *and only when appropriate,* guide him to take responsibility for his own well-being and become a healing channel himself.

# 3

# *Disease and Healing: A General Overview*

## Acute Diseases

By definition these are of short duration and of sharp intensity with a tendency to reach a crisis or peak quickly and then subside—such as a minor gastric upset. Generally, healing given during such conditions results in a quicker, smoother and far less troublesome convalescence and recovery than usual.

## Chronic Diseases

These have a longer duration with no real improvement of the condition. Sometimes chronic conditions require a minimum of 21 treatments before relief is experienced. In case of relapses, continue treatment until relief is well established. Chronic cases may experience a curative 'healing crisis' late in the treatment, or not at all during the course of treatment, but only after 21 treatments.

## Healing Crisis

Also known as *Physical Chemicalization*, this is a release of the physical toxic matter buildup perpetuating the disease. This 'release' is a consequence of the emotional-mental healing taking place—a 'letting go' of the emotional toxins reflected in a dissolving and discharging of the physical toxins. Typically, it takes place on the seventh or eighth or ninth days of treatment. *(For more details refer to the section,* 'Emotions and the Body'.) It is similar to but usually milder than the homeopathic 'curative aggravation'. At this point you may need to explain the process to the healee and *increase the number of treatments* until the crisis passes.

Toxic matter may also be released as through a diarrhoea, a cough and cold, etc. A healing crisis can be minimized or eliminated at the physical level by drinking weak green tea with sugar, and/or magnetized water.

As explored in detail and established in *The Joy of Reiki,* a healing crisis is the reversal of the original disease establishing condition. 'Disease' biochemicals released by our emotional-mental responses, when neither eliminated nor digested, accumulate in the body creating diseased result-states ranging from functional disorders to organic changes and pathology.

When healing takes place, the dissolving of the 'stored' emotional condition results in the release of 'hardened' accumulated biochemicals into the various systems of the body. The body's health intelligence seeks to remove these by a process of 'housekeeping', throwing out the garbage as it were—or a cleansing, eliminating reaction.

*Origins of such disease disorders are always emotional-mental and karmic—a holding on to the blaming-judging of oneself or others.* The deeper the karmic disease, the less the apparent mental-emotional reasons for it. In other words, the healee is unable to identify that there is even any kind of mental-emotional hurt or disorder. (This is exemplified in extreme form, for example, where we find severe birth disabilities—mental-emotional retardation where the individual is not very aware of the suffering. These are very deep karmic disorders.)

The best emotional option is: 'letting go' of judging yourself and 'the other'.

Who is this 'other'? The first 'other' is none other than the fragmented part of ourselves that we have judged and discarded as being 'not me' because that is 'not the real me' or it is the 'bad me'.

And many such fragments and parts live within ourselves, these images of my self—not real, illusory, because these are ever-changing and temporary images of myself. And yet very real because they are my perceptions of my self which prevent my seeing myself as I really am.

These self-images are all stored at the root of the mental body—at the *hara* (*swadisthaan*) region.

Not coincidentally, this is the spiritual power centre, or 'purpose of life area'.

The heaviest blocks in life are guilt energies, and they live at the *hara* region. When we do sufficient healing at the heart and *hara*, our 'purpose of life' is also healed, enabling us to 'live with ourselves' and move on in life.

Forgiving, forgiveness, . . . 'foregoing the act of passing judgement' emotionally on someone for perceived hurts is the key to being healed, to being free of emotional pain—letting go of judgementalism.

This is because if I blame you for my inner state then by retaining it within, I generate and accumulate similar energies within my mental-emotional bodies, developing physical disease ultimately. Thus an attitudinal condition conducive to retention and increase of pain must first exist in some form within me before it manifests externally.

Those with developed diseases where there is no apparent provocation or cause are seen to come from hardened karmic (genetic) results. Even in such cases, the attitudinal markers are in place but they may be more subtle and difficult to examine. The most obvious examples are those of children born with, or suddenly developing, serious disease.

For the purposes of healing, we treat such individuals the same way as we would those who develop the disease after a traceable or more visible chain of cause and effect.

The only practical difference is that the 'degree of difficulty' of the healing is higher under these circumstances, requiring corrective measures at an equivalent vibratory rate.

An 'accident' or surgery is the grossest kind of healing. An accident, particularly, takes place as nature's arrangement to rectify a block arising out of neglect of a condition requiring inner correction.

Just because an accident apparently manifests through the external world does not mean that the cause is external. All causes are first internal. All karma is first internal.

Just as the disease effect comes from our inner response, life also is a mirror and extension of our inner emotional-mental state and condition. The accident is only a sharply delivered disease-result corrective surgery by nature and natural laws.

Similarly, toxic healing agents such as used in chemotherapy, radiation therapy, modern medicinal drugs, certain ayurvedic and herbal medicines are needed to reverse the karmic-genetic results of inner disease.

Therapeutic systems of disease reversal vibrating at higher or more refined frequencies affect disease causes at more subtle levels.

For example, cancer energies may be present in an individual's aura for up to three years and the only signs may be a chaotic emotional condition to which no one would pay much attention, until it actually filters down into the physical body, manifesting as chaotic cell growth.

We find that the typical emotional and attitudinal state of a person suffering from cancer is that he sacrifices many things in order to please others, without receiving any or sufficient recognition. Even though deprived of this response, he is unable to stop or sufficiently modify his unbalanced giving behaviour.

This is the inner chaos between receiving and giving, and reflects in bodily chaos at the area which typically stores such emotions.

Similarly, tuberculosis is born of frustration and inner anger which is suppressed and we see it affecting the thymus (the astral heart chakra); while diabetes comes from deep, old, genetic anger (affecting the spleen chakra and the whole digestive belt—liver, pancreas, solar plexus); kidney disease comes from relationship problems.

Cervical spondylosis arises from an inability to acknowledge mentally what one feels, or what one intuitively knows from the heart—a denial of this felt knowledge.

Sharing this type of knowledge with the healee (the person wanting to be healed) is generally not necessary. This knowledge is for your better understanding of healing.

Whether someone believes in this or not is unimportant—Reiki still works the way it does.

The healing balm for all disease states and conditions is *Usui shiki ryoho*—that unconditional loving Reiki energy which heals unconditionally. We are most grateful to Dr Mikao Usui, for he found again and gave this most powerful of medicines in the universe—medicine that cures all material ills: birth, death, old age and disease.

# 4

# 'Universal Life and Emotional Energy Activity Principles'

In order to further understand how we are affected by emotions, thoughts and so on, we need a way to actually observe and experience their working.

There is no extraordinary technology required for this since this is a matter which is universally demonstrable, and therefore simple methods will suffice.

## Like Attracts Like (The Principle of Affinity or Attraction)

The first principle of the subtle emotional laws of existence is: 'Like attracts like.' We call this the *Principle of Affinity*—whatever we think about or are attentive to, draws, attracts and generates an emotion or thought condition similar to what we are thinking about or feeling.

This is a fundamental principle underlying harmony and order in the universe. In practical terms it means that if we meditate on a past grievance, we start generating and experiencing the negative emotions associated with the event, and although the event may be long gone, the emotions are refreshed, regenerated. The more we meditate on this, more negative energy is generated.

As we give off these vibrations from our energy body, we begin to attract similar vibrations and ultimate confirmation takes place: people with similar complaints and grouses come up to us to confirm that such and such a category of person is indeed worthy of being run-down or criticized or blamed, and so on.

Like the in-laws (outlaws!), best friends (fiends!) who steal husbands/wives—who are helped out and loaned money/things which never come back, and so on. Does this sound familiar?

Such instances are within the experience of all. And by talking this over, receiving sympathy and support (emotional energy) from others, we may feel better having unloaded some of our emotional garbage. We may further feel even better by walking off, or exercising off, our negative energy. Mild exercise expels negative energy from our energy bodies best—the attendant loosening up of tense muscles, especially the shoulder, neck and upper back muscles is de-stressing. Focusing on the breath at the nostrils, intending and taking it down gently down below the navel is also very relaxing.

The practical utility of this principle is, especially for Reiki channels, that the more positive the statements spoken and thought, the more positive life becomes. This is not a matter of 'positive thinking' alone, but *Reiki-empowered* positive thinking, which can effectively change situations radically, as is not possible by other means. This is a matter of confirmed experience and observation by all Reiki channels working sincerely with Reiki.

How does this actually work? This is dealt with by the second Universal Energy Principle.

# 5

# 'Energy Follows Desire and Thought'

## The Principle of Activity

This is the second principle of emotional energy—wherever we direct our desires and thoughts, energy flows in that direction to work on manifesting an external reality according to the thought or desire.

This works whether it is our own energy or universal energy. In our *Reiki Experience*™ seminars we do a simple group experiment to feel our own energies, the pranik energy from our pranik energy body.

First, keep your fingers together, palms slightly cupped. Look at your palms with attention, then turn the palms to face each other keeping them a few centimetres (5–10 cm) apart, ensuring they do not touch at any stage of this experiment.

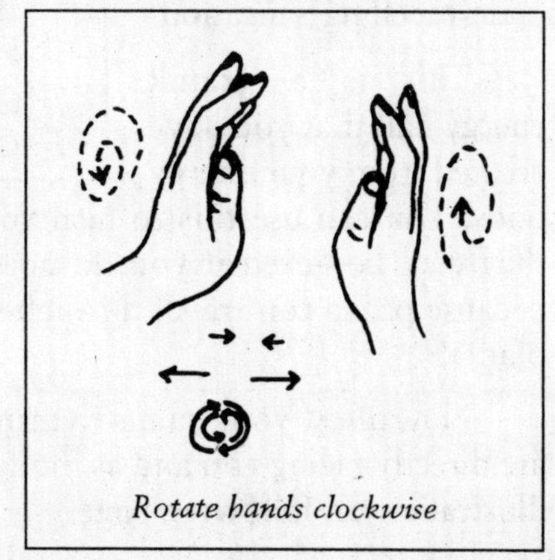
*Rotate hands clockwise*

Then move your hands slowly in a circular movement clockwise five or six times, exactly like a demonstration to a child as to how the wheels of an engine ('choo-choo train') rotate.

After five to six such clockwise movements, reverse the direction, making anti-clockwise movements five or six times only.

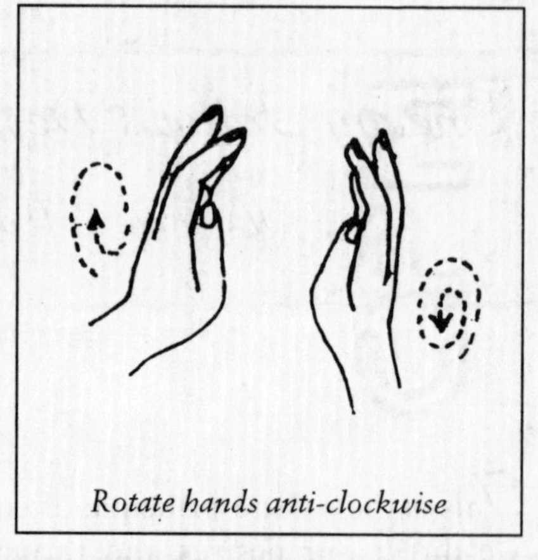

Rotate hands anti-clockwise

Stop the movements, holding your hands still, palms facing each other. Often, by this stage you would feel a tingling, a warmth, a weight, or a pushing-pulling or 'sponge' sensation in your palms.

Without allowing your palms to meet, slowly bring them close to each other and you will usually feel a resistance, pressure, a magnetic repelling sensation.

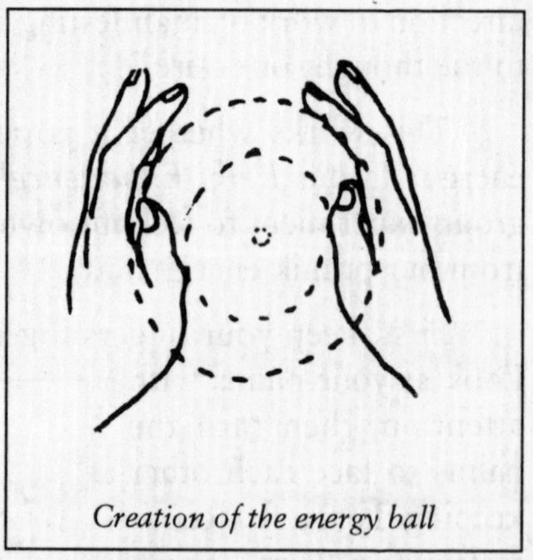

Creation of the energy ball

This is a pranik energy ball that you have created from your energy body. You can use this to heal yourself or others wherever they may be—even if you do not have a Reiki connection, because prana can travel through space to anywhere on this planet.

Now allow your palms to turn upward so that the palms are directly facing you and as though holding something. (See illustration on following page.)

Mentally request the energy ball, *'Please go to my (your own) back heart chakra and open it, thank you.'*

Now slowly allow your palms to return to their original position, facing each other 5–10 centimetres apart. Now slowly bring them close and draw them apart a few times.

What do you notice?

Something is missing. Some sensation you had before is now no longer there.

Further, many would feel a warmth/tingling/pressure in the upper middle back where the back heart chakra is.

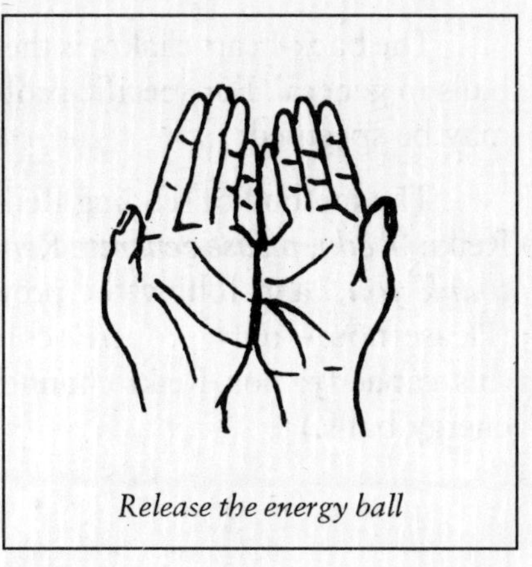

*Release the energy ball*

If not, ask someone else to generate a pranik ball and send it to you, and you do the same for them. This feeling is more pronounced when someone else does this for you.

*Do not generate more than one pranik energy ball in 24 hours if sending it to others.* This is because you may deplete your store of prana and experience a feeling of weakness/exhaustion, etc.

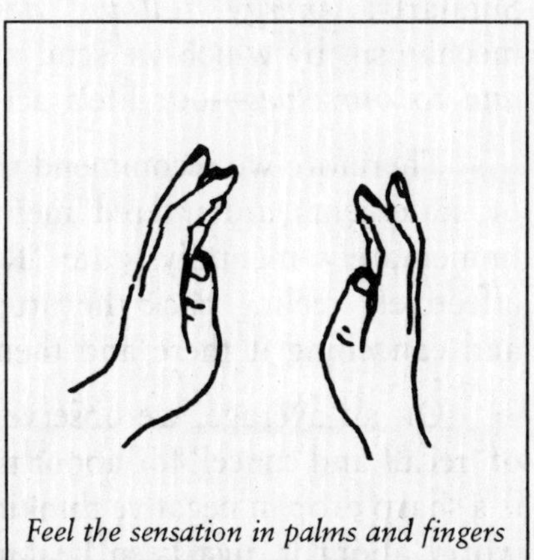

*Feel the sensation in palms and fingers*

You may send as many pranik balls to yourself in a day as you like because you are recycling your own energies within yourself and not being depleted.

The same principle applies to Reiki with a major difference—the Reiki energy does not emanate from your own personal and limited storehouse of energy. It emanates from a limitless supply.

*Therefore, **only** Reiki channels may send* Reiki energy *balls, even at the Reiki first degree level, as a very powerful form of distance healing* .

The **back-heart chakra** is the best place to send the healing balls in general. For specific problems other parts of the body may be specified.

**The method** of sending Reiki balls is to mentally request Reiki: *'Reiki, please generate Reiki healing balls (at my hands), thank you,'* and follow the previously described procedure. (Please note—only properly connected Reiki channels have this capacity; non-Reiki channels can only generate pranik energy balls.)

* * *

Similarly, *energy follows desire and thought* is the mechanism by which we send negative vibrations to others *and to ourselves*—our life's activities.

Therefore we recommend that if any negative thoughts or statements are uttered mentally or verbally, one may immediately mentally state **'Recall and cancel'**, thereby effectively reeling back the utterance and sound vibration and cancelling it there and then.

On an average, we observe that new *Reiki-1s* do a lot of 'recall and cancel' for about two weeks, after which there is a sharp drop in negative thinking itself. If there isn't—don't worry about it, just keep healing yourself especially at the 'heart and hara' position (left hand at hara, right at heart); and at the liver-solar plexus-spleen positions.

We also caution against empathizing or sympathizing with others since this means vibrating at their level; and if they are in pain, it means we too are going to suck up pain energy by the first Principle of Affinity—*Like attracts like.* This connection is made solar plexus-to-solar plexus.

There is a natural tendency for things to come to a balanced state, so when we have less pain, then we tend to suck up others' pain if we sympathize or empathize. This is not a by-product of Reiki—this mechanism exists whether you have Reiki or not.

Because Reiki is a one-way flow of healing energy, while doing healing, we do not 'pick up' others' diseases. However, by 'sympathizing' we activate a solar plexus-to-solar plexus connection as explained, and in this way we can pick up pain and other negative energies.

Instead of this 'non-vegetarian' activity of eating pain directly, we may instead send the person Reiki loving vibrations and wish them well.

In order to do this we may have to unlearn a few cultural patterns which consider it 'good' to 'sympathize' with the other.

This sympathy actually means: 'I am in a superior position to you because I am not suffering that over which you are lamenting and I can give you support while you are unable to deal with the situation yourself.' We may further think, 'Thank heavens, it's happening to someone else, not me.'

The compassionate option for ourselves and the other is to send Reiki loving energy, while expressing loving support in a non-demeaning way.

At a death, we may send Reiki healing to the deceased as well as the family members and say, 'We are praying for the departed soul and for all the family members . . .' We may further express our genuine love for the grieving family members.

We may also gently and lovingly touch them at the back heart chakra, relieving their emotional pain almost instantaneously by re-establishing Reiki loving energy flow within them.

This is the highest service you can perform when faced with another's pain and grief. It is of immediate and practical value, soothing and healing, removing many fears and anxieties. No intellectual theories or platitudes—just simply a direct loving touch, making Reiki available to the one in agony because grief and pain are choking off what little flow of Reiki is available at the embattled heart.

This is unconditional love in action.

# 6

# 'Life Events and Consequent Reactions—Destiny—are Generated by Our Desires'

## The Principle of 'Destiny' or Determination of Life Events

From the previous principles we can see that life events, or our 'destiny' is generated from our desires.

For example, an action taken by us yields a particular result. Our next action depends upon the result already achieved, and our desires coupled with our karmic (activity) bank balance.

These together guide us to the next course of action which entangle us further in a series of action–reaction situations.

Our perceptions are coloured by our karmic patterns. For example, we may be due to get a particular result, then events, coincidences, 'chance' happenings will get together and deliver us a chain of action-reaction so that we get the karmic result.

Efforts to duplicate results of these 'chance' happenings are largely unsuccessful.

If we react to events in a negative way, doing something out of anger, hatred, envy, then the consequences of our acts are similarly tinged with undesirable negative results. 'Good' acts result in positive, beneficial results or accumulation in our karmic bank balance by the principle of *Like attracts like.* Sometimes this may be obscured by apparant injustices in events for which further complex interactions of karma have to be understood.

However, the fundamental principle of karma is the same as Newton's third law of conservation of energy. Simplified, it is—'every action has an equal and opposite reaction'—in other words, 'as you do, so you attract similar results.' And the first action is internal—desires, emotions, thoughts.

This desire-based activity mixed with our karmic bank balance entangles us further in an apparently unending cycle of action-reaction. In order to experience all these desire-based activities one lifetime is insufficient.

Our consciousness needs to be in this universe in different suitable bodily forms to experience these results.

This is the 'karma syndrome' which gives rise to four evils—birth, death, old age and disease. These are evils because they entrap the individual to an illusion which he cannot escape by any measures available in the material experience to which he becomes conditioned.

Changing values of what is right action and wrong action entangle the individual in a cycle of reactive karma. As a Reiki channel how does one deal with 'right' and 'wrong'?

# 7

# 'Perceived Personal Consequences Define Good-Bad, Right-Wrong—While the Most Enforceable Standard of Right-Wrong Prevails'

## The Principle of 'Right' and 'Wrong'

What is right today may be wrong tomorrow or wrong in another place or under different circumstances. The fundamental principle of what is right or good and what is wrong or bad depends on what the individual perceives to be in his best interest or benefit.

Stated simply, 'what's good for me is right, what's not good for me is wrong.' This is the principle that drives individuals, groups, societies and nations.

What is finally 'right' depends on whose standard is most enforceable or whose standard prevails.

This is a verifiable practical reality.

As we experience things changing, responding directly to divine Reiki healing, we come to realize that it is ultimately the spiritual standard which prevails over all odds in the material universe including the 'karma syndrome' and hence that is the most powerful or most correct.

And this standard is enforceable or applicable according to individual desire—if I don't want it then the lower standard will apply.

We have a free will and even if one truly sincere person in purity wants this standard it will manifest . . . as it did on Dr Mikao Usui's desire and request. It is much easier for the rest of us—we only need to ask for it sincerely and connect with it through a bonafide Reiki Master.

The receiving of this standard is made possible by the Divine preparing us to be fit recipients. This is why those who come to Reiki after much suffering, pain, heartbreak, broken relationships and so on can immediately connect with the significance and worth of Reiki and *know instantly* the value of Reiki. That is the price one has paid over many lifetimes in order to receive Reiki.

Getting back to the standards of right and wrong in the material world, we experience that it changes. What is fine today is reversed tomorrow by legislation, and it may not follow the highest spiritual enforceable standard (which has its own repercussions).

*Thus, Reiki channels do not get entangled in the question of deciding what is right or wrong or who is right or wrong as far as healing activity is concerned. Reiki channels just heal—harmonize—everything they come across.* The practical application of this lies in the fifth universal energy principle—the Principle of Healability.

# 8

# 'The Spiritual Energy of Reiki Sufficiently Heals Right-Wrong and the Karma Syndrome'

## The Principle of Healability

In practical terms this means that, for example, when we hear of police atrocities, political corruption and so on, instead of raging helplessly, as Reiki channels, we send healing to all the parties concerned: to the corrupt politicians, to the oppressed and brutalized individuals, and to the oppressors.

And the corrective harmonizing ways and means and results are in Reiki's hands. In many cases, Reiki arranges severe chastisement and punishment for those to whom it is due.

For example, since June 1995 many determined Reiki channels have been sending heartfelt empowered Reiki healing to the political situation in India. In January–February of 1996 there started a political cleansing the likes of which have not been seen before.

Clairvoyantly seen, the shake-up and cleansing is largely Reiki-driven, with Reiki choosing appropriate instruments in its work from time to time in the form of individuals and events. In our practise of clairvoyant counselling of leaders of society we see that their karmic patterns are modified/used by Reiki to grant the request made by Reiki channels.

*And Reiki channels' request is:* that the country's political, socio-economic, bureaucratic, legal, law and order processes become healed, whole and complete—where every individual experiences a peaceful and abun-dant life; that the karma of the citizens of this country be healed sufficiently so that this manifests, and the corrupt learn by personal experience the consequences of their actions and thus be healed from repeating those actions ever again.

Similarly, Reiki channels are sending healing to the parasitic tantriks and other subtle energy bandits who steal one's fortune and lifeforce by misuse and distortion of Universal Energy principles.

These prayers and healings go beyond previous destiny by creating new karma that overrides the past. The difference is that this new karma is being created and organized by divine universal life-force energy at the request of empowered Reiki channels. And such activity ceases to bind the individual to material reactions, contrary to the case with material karma, be it 'good' karma or 'bad' karma.

This will become more evident as increasing numbers of Reiki channels send healing for this, as can you.

*How* the healing takes place or the means used is not in our hands. It is entirely dependent on Divine Will how the objective will be achieved. Therefore, rather than getting entangled in *judging* the right and wrong of any situation, we act to send healing to whatever we come across in our lives—and leave the result to Reiki. *The results are never in our hands although we may request certain results.*

Master Takata liked to say, 'I only have God's healing energy in my hands.' This 'only' can and will harmonize the whole world if we begin by healing our own inner world first by accepting the Reiki healing within and changing internally, as we may need to, in the interest of being whole and complete.

Does this mean we do not ask for results?

No. It does not mean we cannot ask for results. We ask for results by way of 'healing', 'harmony', 'abundance', for persons and situations to become 'whole and complete', free from pain and in a state of happiness. We do not get caught up or sucked into judging a particular case or the individuals involved.

We may feel internally that something requires healing, or we want that it should be healed—that is alright. Request and be committed to healing in that direction.

Therefore, we send healing to the victim of a crime as well as to the criminal, praying, requesting that all concerned be 'healed, whole and complete'. That is all.

Reiki heals and harmonizes, whether the situation is 'right' or 'wrong,' and whatever the karma may be. Thus the *karma syndrome* with its attendant fourfold evils of birth-death-old age-disease is also gradually healed, dissolved. Otherwise there is no sense and no meaning to the term and goal of 'being whole and complete'.

Another meaning of 'whole and complete' is: 'holy'. If we heal ourselves and whatever we come across, the inner and outer worlds are both healed, holy.

How may we better understand this better? This is dealt with by the sixth principle.

## Food and Diet

'As your self-healing progresses, you will be drawn more and more to simpler forms of food and diet. As your karma heals and your vibratory rate increases you will function best with more 'refined' types of food fuel—light, simple and simply prepared food.

'You may think, "Oh, my digestion became worse after doing a couple of years of Reiki!"

'The reality is that your system has become more purified and hence requires more of what is known as the *sattvic* foods, or foods in the mode of goodness such as fresh fruit, lightly cooked vegetables with a minimum of chillies, spices and oils. In any event, what you find most comfortable for yourself in the matter of diet should be followed.

'It is no good lamenting, "I can't digest my evening double whisky and steak and potatoes".'

'The purified digestion will reject this diet eventually and this is not a sign that you are worse off, but rather that your physical bodily system is naturally reflecting the purification that acceptance of Reiki brings.'

'The ultimate purified diet in a natural way for some or a few may become just air and water and Reiki—but don't try this artificially of course!'

—*Teachings of the Fourth Grandmaster*

# 9

# 'The Physical Body and Life Events are Mirrors Reflecting Our Inner Situation and Condition'

## The Principle of Expansion of Consciousness

It is common experience that when faced with any kind of external threat, our body reacts on its own. For example, we may feel something 'fluttering' in our solar plexus or abdominal region.

Certain biochemicals, hormones are released by the body in response to the perceived threat and these energize us to take some defensive or offensive action.

At the end of the crisis, there is a 'let-down' in the tension, the excitement, and an opposite 'low' state may occur. This is known as 'shock'—blood sugar becomes low, one may feel cold and so on. However, one usually recovers rapidly from such trauma suffering little or no after-effects.

However, when we respond to events and situations as though our life is threatened, and we do not get an 'end of crisis' signal, the body keeps generating the action-stimulating biochemicals. When these are neither eliminated nor absorbed (digested) in the system, they accumulate in certain body parts, tissues, organs and systems according to predisposition.

'Indigestion is the mother of all disease,' says ayurvedic science. Emotional indigestion can also lead to physical 'indigestion', an accumulation of stressful (toxic) biochemicals which first alter the functioning of the organ or system, and then finally effect physical changes in the organs or systems in order to compensate for the distortion.

This could become 'settled' or established chronic disease. External measures such as surgery may become necessary, but surgery will generally not create conditions for a permanent cure. At the same time it may very well be a life-saving procedure, buying time as it were, so that we can heal the inner emotional causes for the external disease.

Emotions and attitudes are reflected in our body by the release and creation of analogous biochemicals. When these accumulate sufficiently, there is disease.

This is the way that our body reflects our inner condition and state. In the language of Reiki, you will learn that different parts of the body store different emotions, different attitudes in biochemical disease form.

As you develop experience in Reiki healing of others, you will receive confirmation through their bodies that disease has a common emotional language that is universal.

And just as the body is an expansion of our inner state, the whole world, in terms of events that take place with us, is an expansion of our inner state as well.

The world is a mirror of our inner condition and it reflects what we have within. Thus world events are made up of the combined interactions of all the inner states of all living beings. If we look for being whole and complete and happy exclusively for ourselves, it is bound to be insufficient.

In order to be whole and complete, the whole world also must be healed. The first step is to heal oneself, one's inner world and the external will also change.

How?

One of our Reiki Masters gave a beautiful example: 'Only one pearl in the whole necklace needs to shift, and all the pearls will shift . . . you be that pearl. Heal and shift yourself and everything will shift.'

This is because each living being is connected with the common beautiful thread of Reiki, the Reiki channels only more so and in greater awareness.

And when such a being shifts internally, the external universe, the environment, also shifts and changes to accommodate this shift. It may be very slight, but it is there. These shifts are magnified and very visible in the lives of Reiki channels who have healed themselves in a significant and major way.

Such is the common experience of all Reiki channels. After their Reiki connection and self-healing they find their social circle changes. Forgotten figures, friends from the past reappear to re-establish old connections, complete some karmic transactions while the present social circle may have many new faces rather suddenly. Relationships take on a new and different meaning.

As Reiki channels further advance in their self-healing, their physical environment changes. They shift jobs or houses, or re-build/re-decorate their living environment—sometimes very extensively.

Their work, business or occupation may change or expand or move in a different positive direction.

All this takes place within a relatively short period of time—within six months to a year of their having done Reiki-2 with us, following our methods with commitment and dedication. Abundance immediately manifests in Reiki channels' lives—first internally, then externally.

Universally acting mechanisms work to deliver and carry this to the individual to whom the Divine has promised, 'He who is devoted to Me and My work, and who works with Me and My energies, he who is bathed in My energies and in whom I reside and he who resides in Me, and to whose welfare I am devoted in reciprocity, to such a one *I personally* carry and convey what he lacks and protect what he has.'*

In the cut-and-dried system of karmic reaction-action of life, the Divine now takes an active personal interest in he who is chanelling Reiki with dedication.

* Bhagvad Gita 9.22

# 10

# The 'Attitude of Gratitude'

After the Reiki initiations (attunements) the healing process rests entirely on the grace of the Divine Universal Consciousness and one's internal attitude. In order to be properly placed internally, one must *request and accept* the healing Reiki energy out of one's *free will* or desire.

This applies to healing oneself or channeling healing to another—the 'healee'. *Therefore, as a preliminary general rule for Reiki-1 channels, healing may be given only when the other requests it.*

The healing channel (you) must invoke or be in an 'attitude of gratitude' before starting a treatment or ending it. Before starting the healing treatment, you may internally state or reflect while in a receptive frame of consciousness, or *be* in an attitude of gratitude where words are not necessary. If there is doubt *(and there always is in the beginning stages)*, the formal invocation is:

*'I thank myself for being here. I thank Reiki for being here. I thank* (healee's name/your name if you are doing self-treatment) *for being here. Reiki please make* (healee's name/your name if doing self-treatment) *healed whole and complete. So it is. Thank you. Thy/Divine Will be done.'*

This is the *opening attitude of gratitude* consciousness before commencing any treatment.

At the end of a healing session, the *closing attitude of gratitude* consciousness is:

'(Healee's name/your name) *is healed, whole and complete. So it is. Thank you. Thy/ Divine Will be done. I thank Reiki, I thank* (healee's name or your name if doing self-treatment), *I thank myself.'*

We may note here that while Reiki is not a religious system, by observation and definition it is a 'spiritual' system of healing, not limited by religious practices or faiths. The energy may be impersonal whereas the 'energetic', the Source, may be personal.

Each of us may be inclined to approach this either at the personal level or impersonal level, referring to divinity as 'God's Will' or 'Thy Will' as we may prefer. 'Thy' can be an address to the energy as well as the person.

There is no contradiction or clash of any kind between 'personalism' and 'impersonalism'—or even atheism or any other 'ism', as when applied to Reiki.

If we have no direct experience in the matter and do not wish to accept the terms 'God' or 'Divine' Will, we may substitute the term 'Universal Consciousness' or 'Universal Heart'.

It is not necessary to have faith in God, or a Supreme Divine Being in order to receive Reiki benefits. At the same time we should not be critical of those who believe or accept Reiki is coming from a 'divine' source because their acceptance may be from purified direct perception and realization.

Just as in many things in life we accept 'authoritative' statements as having weight and value, similarly if advanced

Reiki channels having all good qualities are making such statements, they are not doing so lightly.

We may accept them as having weight, subject to confirmation.

It is just like hearing the chemistry professor who may say, '. . . when we mix two colourless gases (hydrogen and oxygen) and carefully introduce a lighted taper (a flame) to the mixture, it will create an explosion and water.'

If we are very sure of ourselves and our level of knowledge, and having freshly stepped into his class, we may dismiss the professor as a madman. And yet in the laboratory the professor would be seen to be factually right, and we, quite the foolish ones.

The professors of Reiki (the Grandmasters) too are perfectly scientific, having no time for fairy tales or imagination. They work in the laboratory of life and life experiences itself—both, the subtle and gross.

The system of verification here is also direct experience—purified direct experience which radically changes the life of individuals.

It is verifiable by anyone who follows the process and just does their self-healing sincerely. The reality of this is confirmed again and again by Reiki channels committed to their self-healing and self-development. *A person not connected to Reiki or a person who is connected, but has not healed himself is not an authority on the subject.*

Thus, such a person who is being judgemental-critical here will create the greatest of obstacles to his progress in self-healing, self-development. Avoid such criticism totally, and if one has so criticized—'recall and cancel', and use the *Divine Reiki Light* method to heal this.

No material force in the universe can retard or stop Reiki—only offense against those who are spiritually connected. The higher the offense, the more difficult it is to digest.

Spiritualists in the past have classified this as the basic and fundamental first offense—criticism against the spiritually connected. In the Vedas this is known as *'sadhu ninda'*—criticism against those who are rightly placed, the spiritually empowered and connected.

It does not matter whether the 'offendee' (person against whom offense has been committed) belongs to a particular religious group or to none.

A person in or out of a religious group may be spiritually connected and empowered regardless of his religious affiliation, political belief and personal faith in various matters—or of our limited opinion of him. (By its nature, 'spiritual' means 'not limited or bound by material considerations'.)

The result of offense is immediate—a *temporary shutting down* of the Reiki flow in the chakras of the individual, a constriction of the person's aura, an immediate pulling in of negative grey-brown-black-red energies, dissipating abundant energies.

Why is this?

This is an example of the first two laws of Universal Energy in action—*energy follows thought* and *like attracts like.* Laws that are more potent where Reiki channels are involved.

Criticism-judgementalism means that we send 'not-love' to the individual. This 'not-love' sent out also attracts 'not-love', resulting in a severe reduction of Reiki flow due to the constriction of the pathways in the energy body.

This is the reason that one of the most well-known and greatest of Reiki channels of all time, Jesus Christ, categorically and firmly instructed his students—'you shall not judge others, lest you be judged and call judgement upon yourself.'

If we can spiritually digest the act of judgementalism, little or no ill effect takes place.

If we cannot digest the offense, in other words if the magnitude of offense is great—the 'offendee' being spiritually more advanced than the offender—then, the reaction will manifest in the form of a physical-emotional 'cleansing' or a life-situation 'cleansing'—at the financial, emotional, professional fronts. This means a throwing up and out of the accumulated negativities within.

At the extreme, we have seen the self-important materially rich becoming reduced to relative penury in a very short period of time *directly* due to this spiritual offense.

Reiki channels need to be very careful here because it is a waste of time and healing energy. Where such 'cleansings' take place due to offense, the Reiki channel may be thinking he is actually progressing, wiping out karmic reactions, while the reality is otherwise.

The reality is that he has slipped back into uncomfortable contact with material nature, away from Reiki—marking time, suffering the pangs of material nature again, thinking he is progressing. This is soothing illusion making the discomfort somewhat bearable.

This is very evident especially where such a person continues to be critical-judgemental of others.

However, because Reiki is unconditional loving energy, soon the flow will get re-established. The diversion away from Reiki may be necessary to teach us something. It is better if we learn this by understanding it through intelligence rather than personal experience. But even if we are in such a position where we experience this personally, there is no long-term loss.

Ask forgiveness using the *Divine Reiki Light,* heal the offense, leave it behind and move on with direct understanding in the light of this experience.

## Opening Attitude of Gratitude

- **'I thank myself for being here . . .'** addresses the pure essential part of myself that is chanelling the healing.
- **'I thank Reiki for being here . . .'** addresses and invokes Reiki directly and affirmatively.
- **'I thank (healee's name/my name) for being here . . .'** addresses by its given name, the personality and ego that requires healing, whether it is I or the other.
- **'Reiki please make (healee's name) healed, whole and complete . . .'** addresses the healing request.
- **'So it is . . .'** is an absolute and positive affirmation of the request, empowering it with Reiki energy through speech.
- **'Thank you, Thy/Divine Will be done. . .'** we express our gratitude and affirms further that the healing request is empowered by superior Divine Will through Reiki and therefore unstoppable and invincible, while results are ultimately according to Divine Will or the Will of God, or Universal Consciousness ('Thy Will').

> 'As you progress in healing and in your own spiritual evolution, your inner guidance and will shall gradually coincide and overlap more and more with Divine Will so that you naturally function in increasing harmony with the Divine. Thus, the will of the *self-realized Reiki channel* is non-different from Divine Will. *But don't be in a rush to think your will is the Will of the Divine—that you are or can become the Supreme Divine*—that is gross foolishness!'

## Closing Attitude of Gratitude

- **'(Healee's name) is healed whole and complete, so it is, thank you . . .'** positively declares and affirms the healee to be healed and indicates that the Reiki flow for the purpose of healing the designated healee may now cease. (Even so, the flow of Reiki never completely stops except at the time of the living being transiting from this body, when it pauses for between three to five minutes to allow the transition, before starting again.)
- **'Thy/Divine Will be done . . .'** declares that the healing is according to Divine Will and therefore unstoppable and invincible, and that the final results are in accordance with Divine Will.
- **'I thank Reiki, I thank (healee's name), I thank myself . . .'** expresses gratitude to Reiki for the healing, as well as for the extra healing that comes to us every time we channel healing for anyone

(including ourselves). This is every Reiki channel's automatic 'commission' for chanelling healing. Clairvoyantly seen, a precise 20 per cent accrues to the Reiki channel. (In *addition* to this, the 'energy exchange' is essential.) Gratitude is also expressed to 'myself', that pure part of 'me' that channels the Reiki healing, and also to the healee for giving the opportunity to convey the healing.

> In your own healing the 'Closing' Attitude of Gratitude (AOG) does not mean that Reiki stops flowing for you. It means that you have concluded this particular healing session for yourself, detaching yourself from it, and Reiki will now flow in 'maintenance' mode for you.
>
> At the same time, when you make the closing affirmation—that you are healed—it is a very powerful statement carrying much Reiki energy to establish that affirmation's result.
>
> At least once every 24 hours you should make the closing AOG. (We suggest you do this on waking. You may immediately open again after that if you so desire.)

## Summary—The Attitude of Gratitude

If my name is Renoo, before starting the healing (Opening) I will say: *'I thank myself for being here, I thank Reiki for being here, I thank Renoo for being here, Reiki please make Renoo healed whole and complete. So it is. Thank you. Thy (or Divine) Will be done.'*

For closing the healing session for myself (Renoo) I will declare: *'Renoo is healed whole and complete. So it is. Thank you, Thy (or Divine) Will be done. I thank Reiki, I thank Renoo, I thank myself.'*

For healing yourself you would insert and substitute your own name in the Opening and Closing Attitudes of Gratitude (AOG).

Thus:

'I thank Reiki for being here, I thank myself for being here, I thank (your name) for being here, Reiki please make (your name) healed, whole and complete. So it is. Thank you. Thy (or Divine) Will be done.'

For closing the healing session for yourself, declare: '(Your name) is healed, whole and complete, so it is, thank you, Thy (or Divine) Will be done. I thank Reiki, I thank myself, I thank (your name).'

For healing others, I will similarly insert the other's name in the Attitude of Gratitude, opening and closing.

Before healing Madhu, I will say for the opening of the healing session: *'I thank myself for being here, I thank Madhu for being here, I thank Reiki for being here, Reiki please make Madhu healed, whole and complete. So it is. Thank you. Thy/Divine Will be done.'*

For closing the healing session for Madhu I will declare: *'Madhu is healed whole and complete. So it is. Thank you. Thy/Divine Will be done. I thank Reiki, I thank Madhu, I thank myself.'*

'The Attitude of Gratitude is not just a set of words—it is an internal position. It is a real and spontaneous state of consciousness arising from awareness of the flow of joy from the heart.

'In the beginning we may not be sincere. We may not even know what it really means to be grateful. Even so, Reiki is very generous and says, "It doesn't matter even if you don't mean what you say—just say the words or think it and I'll accept it as though you meant it with full sincerity. . . ." There are no limits to the love which flows from the cosmic heart.'

— *Teachings of the Fourth Grandmaster of Reiki*

# 11

# Working with the 'Attitude of Gratitude' Consciousness

The 'Attitude of Gratitude' consciousness may be in different words or images *but the intention is important. 'Thy (or Divine) Will be done'*: God, (the Divine, Supreme Source of all sources) and the Reiki healing energy are invoked for very good reasons:

- This is to remind oneself that one is *only* a *channel or instrument* for the healing flow. The object is to eliminate the false consciousness that one is the 'doer'. Divine or Superior Will controls the healing flow. The consciousness that 'I am the doer' is called *'ahankaar'* or the false ego identification of being the actual doer of the healing. *Such an attitude blocks one's own progress and the conveying of healing*. Be reminded that we are healed, whole and complete only due to *Divine Grace—Reiki.*

- The second reason is that this statement *detaches* you from the *results* of the healing. *The healing result is never in your hands—only the Divine healing energy is.* Desired results may not come immediately because of many individual factors and when it does it is always ultimately by Divine Will. However, Reiki channels do not take this as a license to push responsibility for their own lack of effort on to Reiki. They do their work to the best of their ability and leave the results to the Divine.

So, while we may be *detached* from results, at the same time we must be *committed* to results. This means correcting all that which prevents results, starting with *becoming aware of the blocks caused by our own attitudes and behaviour*—especially the action of the false ego: 'I am the doer'.

*Never take up a healing as a challenge* to your sense of being 'the healer', or as a challenge to Reiki.

*Never doubt that Reiki works, even if the desired results may not be immediately visible. Reiki has her own intelligence and works accordingly. Master Takata used to say, 'Results are not in my hands—only God's healing energy is.'*

*Results* of the healing also depend on the individual healee's commitment to *rectify what may be wrong or blocked within himself and his attitudes.* The *healee* (person being healed) must also have an attitude of gratitude for what he is receiving and *accept* being healed.

Therefore, there must also be an *exchange of energy* for the time spent by you, the healer, for channelling the healing.

Dr Usui experienced this reality after devoting many years of healing at a beggars' camp in Kyoto where he found that they had no value nor gratitude for the healing because there had been a lack of energy exchange.

As Dr Usui learned from this experience that *something that is received free is worth only as much as the person pays for it* in terms of *energy-exchange,* which in the beggars' case was: *nothing.*

If the healing costs nothing in terms of energy—either in service energy or money (which is accumulated energy of our work), *the healing cannot be totally successful.*

*If the healee is indebted to the healing channel, he may develop resentment, lack of gratitude and disrespect for the healer or Reiki, which immediately blocks healing results. Therefore, the healer must be fully aware of this mechanism and avoid doing anything that promotes such a response in the healee.* Such blocks in the healing process only serve to delay the healing and extend the suffering of the healee. As Reiki channels making healing available to the healee, we must harmonize everything so that the healing process is given every opportunity to be successful.

*The energy exchange may be simple, but appropriate.* For example, you may give healing to parents, children, friends, well-wishers and others without anything more than a simple *request for healing* or *acceptance of healing* from them before the healing, and a natural, simple expression of gratitude and thanks from them after the healing.

- If, while following this, you find that the individual has no value for the healing, then send *only distance healing* according to the methods explained further, including an intention in the Reiki Box that *the healee has accepted being healed and wants to be healed.*

The Attitude of Gratitude and the Energy Exchange are both reflections of an inner attitude. Money, service, expressions of gratitude received as energy exchange for *your time* should be appropriate, always keeping in view the other's capacity to pay, never denying healing on the basis that the other cannot pay high fees. *The divine Reiki healing energy cannot be valued in material terms.*

Reiki healing is beyond any material pricing, while your time and services and skill at creating the best healing support conditions may certainly and very properly be assessed as having a certain money value.

* * *

'If someone is thankful, and expresses it—isn't that sufficient energy exchange? Why is there so much stress on payment? Something divine should be free.'

In general, in the case of immediate family we may accept this because within this category there is much karmic debt to each other, and even if there is not much sincerity from the other side, it does not matter very much in practical terms.

In the case of others including friends, associates (and sometimes relatives as well), a socially correct but casual 'thank you' is not sufficient and often masks an attitude of 'ingratitude'—which is offensive and will actually block the healing results. One of the side-effects of this may well be that your fledgling experiential faith in Reiki is shaken.

When someone 'pays' in money or services for the healing, there is automatically an idea of 'value' in their estimation which also translates to 'respect'. They no longer treat the healing, or you, casually. Some seriousness is there. This is particularly true where an elder relative reminds you they dandled you on their knees and changed your nappies! This is a difficult one—so at least ask to be treated to tea and sandwiches by them! Or, send distance healing, including an intention that their attitude has changed.

As a representative of Reiki, making healing energy available, you have great value. By selling yourself short, as it were, out of some sense of embarrassment or emotional unease you are also selling Reiki short in your own estimation as well as the other person's. *Energy follows thought*, *Like attracts like*—be careful, understanding the interplay of these mechanisms in such circumstances.

We have experience of people taking the healing with the attitude they are doing the healer a great favour by allowing them to give them Reiki healing! Clearly, there is no question of gratitude from such persons even if they mouth the words, 'Thank you'.

In order for healings to be successful for them, energy exchange is essential, and at a level which makes them sit up and pay attention. However, you have to be very balanced here so that you are not acting out of a false ego, but as a compassionate Reiki channel who knows the real and practical value of Reiki healing and who has the confidence that, 'Reiki always works'. There is no need to be greedy. All abundance manifests in Reiki channels' lives very quickly as they heal themselves and others.

Another major reason for the necessity of energy exchange is that *you must be committed to the healing.* We observe that without the mechanism of energy exchange most Reiki healers tend to be casual in their healing, forgetting the Fourth Principle of Reiki—*Just for today I shall do my work honestly.* The energy-exchange protects you and focuses you on doing your work properly in making the healing available *and being committed to results.* This comes naturally with the energy exchange system—the Grandmasters of Reiki did not put forward this practical principle of Reiki lightly.

In our own healing practise, we charge differently for the same type of healing from persons of different socio-economic backgrounds, each according to their capacity and ability. *But charge we must in some form or other*—even if it be for the person to 'spend' time praying for us and for our work to progress. The Reiki healing is priceless, but the healer's time, overheads for providing the healing and various other expenses involved are not 'free'.

The healee is automatically indebted to the healer unlimitedly because what he is receiving through the agency of the healer is virtually 'without price and unpriceable'—it cannot be valued materially. However, by a *token payment of energy exchange* this unlimited debt is taken care of.

'Free', on the other hand, may be a selling gimmick for which you pay in some other hidden way, or it may be worthless, or a means to cheat or manipulate. That which is beyond pricing, unpriceable, or priceless is never 'free' in the sense that the uninformed may understand it. In order to receive benefits from the Divine, the healee must be able to *give* of his energies as well so that by the principle of *Like attracts like* he is able to absorb the Reiki healing, after creating some space by giving.

This is practical reality for the understanding of Reiki channels. *As far as the healee is concerned,* if you simply and calmly point out that you are charging for your time, the overheads and your expenses for reversing problems, whereas the healees in general may have spent vast amounts of energy and money unsuccessfully pursuing this goal, the relatively small energy exchange is a non-issue.

There is no need to get into justifications, pontifications or arguments—no helplessness, please!

*In a confrontationist situation*—Just centre yourself at the heart, mentally balance their chakras (and yours if needed!), use the appropriate *Instant Healing* techniques as summarized in the appendix. The persons will be peaceful in a few moments, picking up the vibrations coming from you.

# 12

# *Reiki Healing—Sequence, Time, Emergencies*

## Sequence

The given sequence of full-body Reiki is listed according to the natural Reiki flow. There are 26 points where Reiki is given. Each leg has 5 points and if we include the points for both legs, effectively we have 31 point positions where to give Reiki.

## Healing Time

The recommended time spent at each point for healing is three minutes for **Adults**. Thus a full-body Reiki session would last about 90 minutes.

**Children and Teenagers** require much less time. For infants and young children, the total Reiki time is 10 to 15 minutes. Also, while giving infants and young children Reiki, the hand would cover more than one point simultaneously because their bodies are smaller. Children and teenagers' self-healing of between 15 minutes to 30 minutes a day is sufficient unless there are serious health or life-situation problems, or special events (exams, competitions, etc.) requiring extra healing.

Children below eight years of age may not receive attunements as their energy fields are not developed sufficiently and premature attunement may be harmful.

## Emergencies

In an emergency or when treating a specific acute problem, you may give Reiki at the problem area (even if it is not part of the listed positions).

Then also give Reiki to the back heart chakra, solar plexus, knees; and at any other positions as may be required according to individual situations and specific feedback.

## Cardiac Emergencies

Avoid giving Reiki at the front heart chakra if a person has or is suspected to have an *acute* heart condition accompanied by any symptoms such as moderate to severe pain in the chest (and left arm or elbow), sweating, nausea, palpitations, etc.

- You may immediately give Reiki at the back heart chakra with one hand and the front (or back) solar plexus chakra with the other hand.
- Mentally request Reiki to open healee's back heart chakra and to keep it open.
- Reiki-2 channels may mentally chant the names of the symbols without drawing them mentally in an emergency only. If a Reiki-2 channel is very much in Reiki consciousness (as in an emergency), just the intention or desire or inner appeal to Reiki will cause the symbols to reach the healee.
- When the healee is relieved, continue Reiki at the back heart chakra with one hand and give Reiki to the knees with the other. You may need to go back to the heart-solar plexus region again if pain continues. *Follow your inner guidance.*
- The procedure as described, done by Reiki-1 channels in hospital conditions, has directly saved lives and facilitated recovery with *minimal or no*

*damage* to the heart, with the essential help of the hospital intensive care facilities. The Reiki procedure described is effective, whatever the cause or wherever the site of the problem may be.

- *Do not be afraid of giving Reiki under such conditions. . . .* Reiki will automatically flow *as needed* because the healee draws as much healing as needed—the Reiki channel only makes healing 'available'.
- Severe indigestion or cervical spondylosis pains can mimic heart pains. Follow the described procedure in such an event in any case.

NOTE

*Seek medical aid promptly in all doubtful conditions.*

## DEPRESSION

'At some time or other we may feel disheartened, let down, depressed that things are not working out properly for us.'

'We understand from this that some negative energies are surfacing and will soon be gone. This will take place faster if we help it along by increasing our self-healing, understanding what it is that we have to let go.'

'Therefore, it is a time to be internally pleased or time to celebrate the departure of old pains now released for being healed even though externally we may show manifestations of grief, pain and sorrow.'

'At this time we may want to be with ourselves and receive the loving energies of Reiki in privacy.'

'This is also being in Reiki consciousness.'

—*Teachings of the Fourth Grandmaster*

# 13

# Reiki Consciousness

Being in 'Reiki Consciousness' means experiencing awareness of Reiki, being in awareness of the flow of Reiki love within and outside, being thankful that Reiki flows through you in great volume, expanding your consciousness of joy.

It means having the capacity to make available the harmonizing and healing touch of Reiki to whomever and whatever you see and hear and experience—to whatever you come across in life.

Reiki consciousness means sending healing, making Reiki available especially to those who have hurt you the most, those whom you dislike or resent the most, the so-called 'enemies'—because in sending healing to them, *you actually dissolve and become free of your karmic debt of receiving negative emotional energies of hate, envy, anger, 'enmity', from them.* It is in your interest.

Do not continue to think, 'they don't deserve the benefits of Reiki', because it is to *your* benefit, sending them healing.

In the process of making healing available to the other, you become relieved of the necessity of vibrating at the negative energy levels of anger, hatred, envy, enmity. The outflow of Reiki love protects you.

## Reiki Healing Sequence and the Reiki 26/31 Point Positions

- *Open and close with the Attitude of Gratitude*
- *Do not cross feet/legs while healing self/others*

### Front Body

1. Eyes
2. Temples
3. Forehead/back of the head (ajña chakra, 'third eye')*
4. Ears
5. Back of the head (occipital lobes)
6. Throat and thyroid glands *
7. Thymus gland
8. Heart *
9. Solar plexus *
10. Liver and gall bladder
11. Lung tips
12. Spleen and pancreas
13. Hara/sacral plexus*
14. Spermatic cords/ ovaries
15. Thighs
16. Knees
17. Calves
18. Ankles
19. Feet soles

(Front and back, using both hands for each point on each leg)

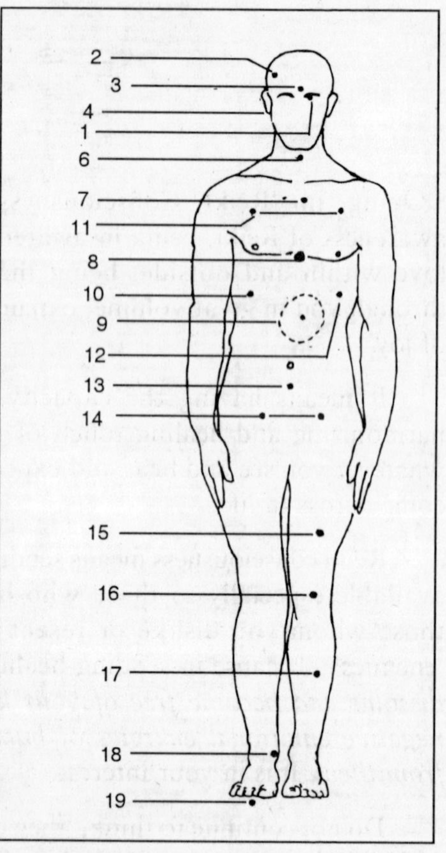

## Back Body

20. Shoulders
21. Thymus
22. Heart
23. Solar plexus
24. Kidneys
25. Hara/sacral plexus
26. Root chakra or base of spine*

The seven major chakras are marked *

1. Crown
2. Ajna or third eye
3. Throat
4. Heart
5. Solar plexus
6. Hara
7. Root or base or *mooladhaar*

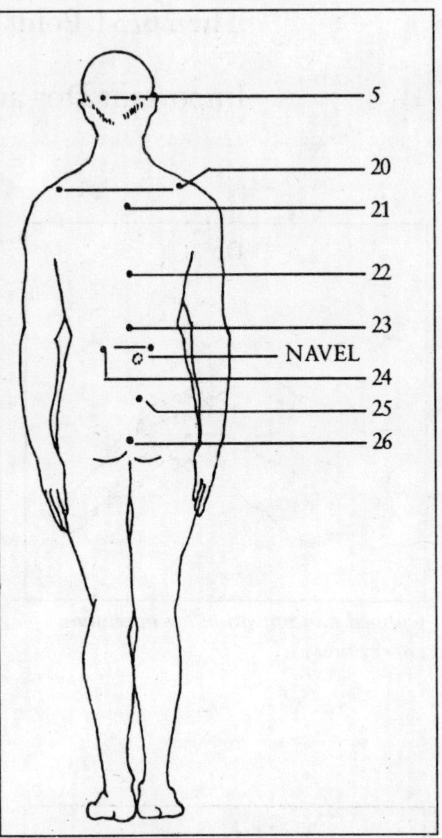


26 points + 5 extra leg positions make a total of 31 point-positions.

**Full-body Reiki Time**

| | | |
|---|---|---|
| Adults | : | 90 minutes |
| Teenagers | : | 30 minutes |
| Children | : | 15 minutes |

*Please Remember*

Reiki is never given on top of the head (the crown/*sahasraar* chakra) nor at the navel.

# The 26/31 Point Positions

## Important Dos and Don'ts

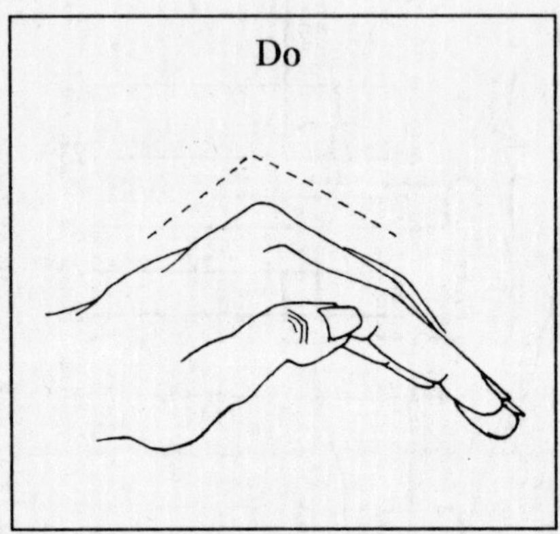


*Cupped hand position for maximum energy flow.*

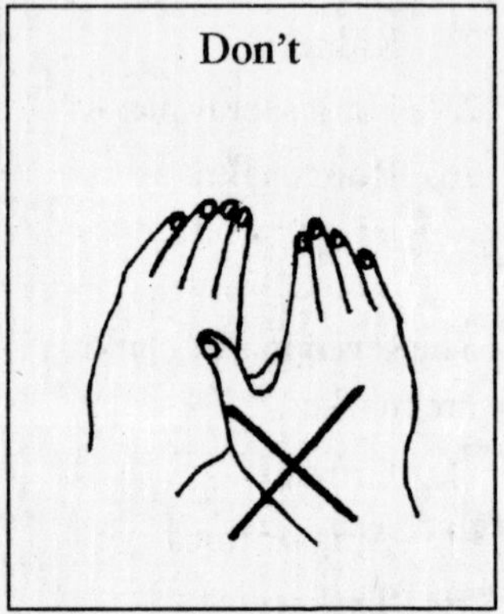


*Never give Reiki with thumb apart from the fingers.*

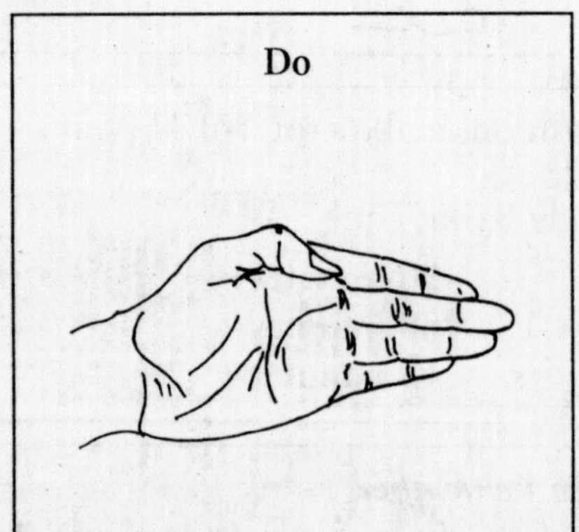


*Thumb may be folded in, especially at the throat position.*

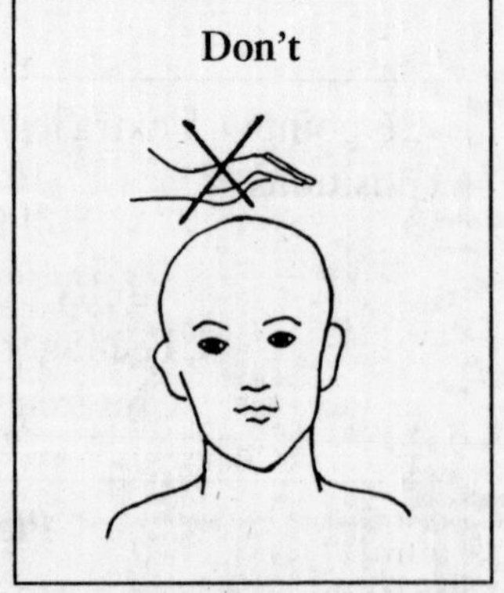


*Never give Reiki on top of the head (crown chakra).*

# The 26/31 Point Positions

## Front Body Positions

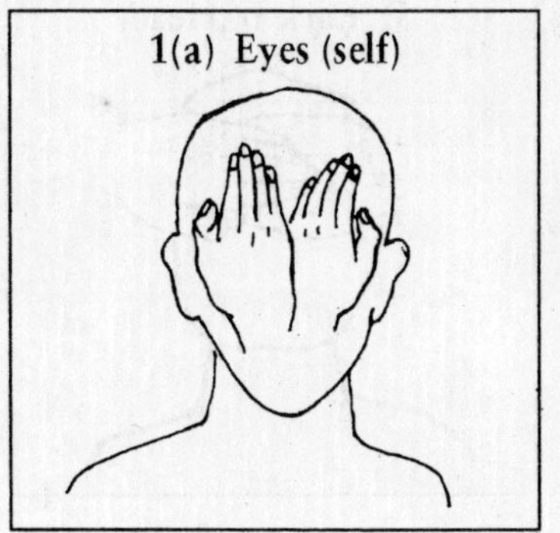
1(a) Eyes (self)

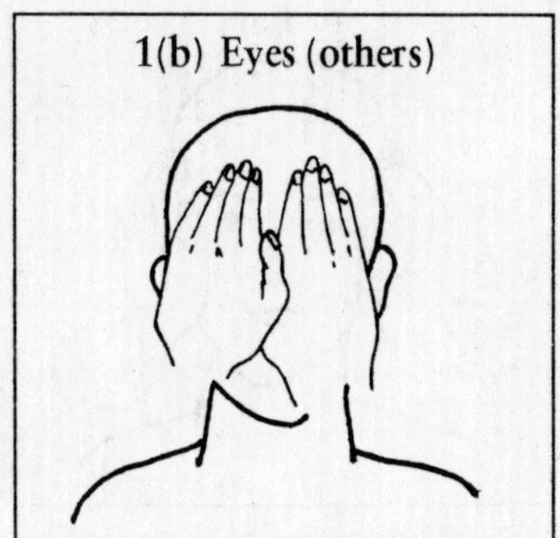
1(b) Eyes (others)

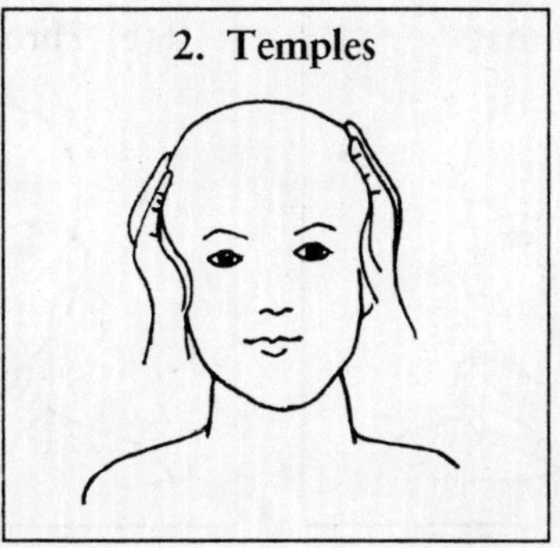
2. Temples

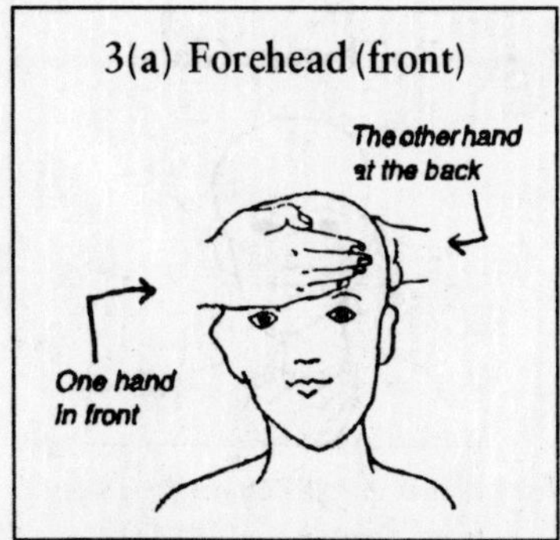

3(a) Forehead (front)

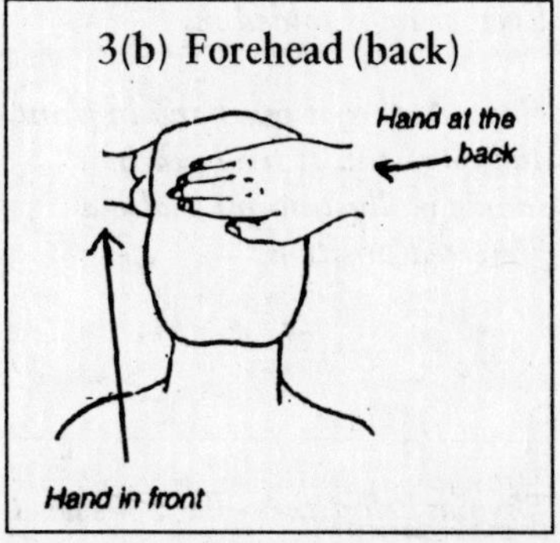

3(b) Forehead (back)

## The 26/31 Point Positions

### Front Body Positions (continued)

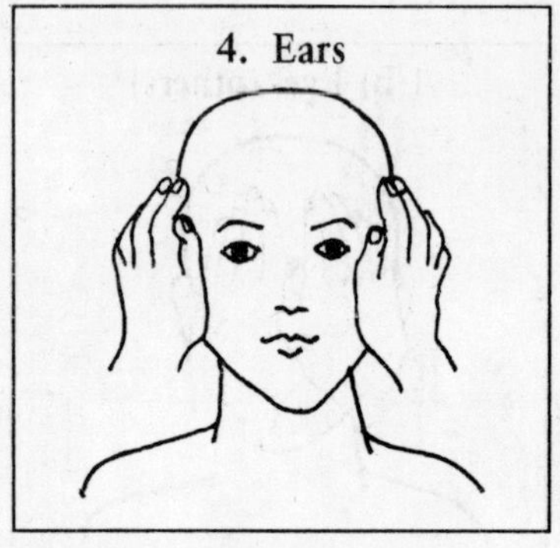
4. Ears

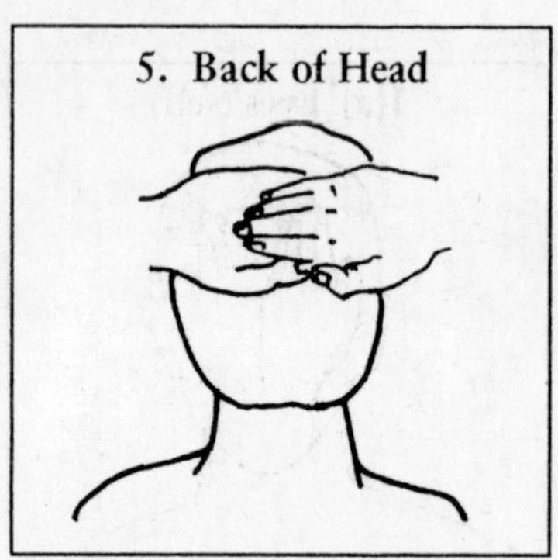
5. Back of Head

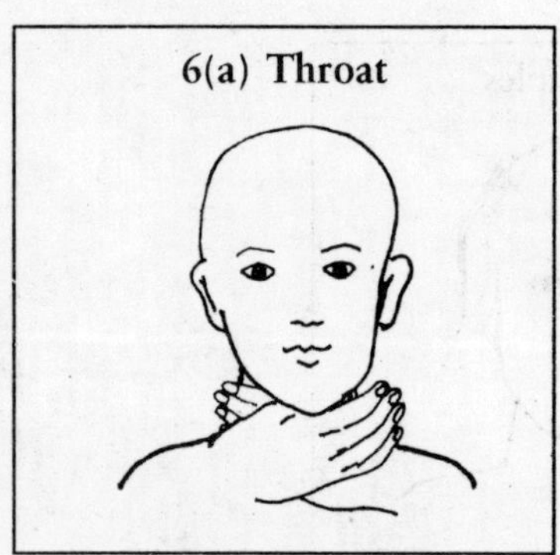
6(a) Throat

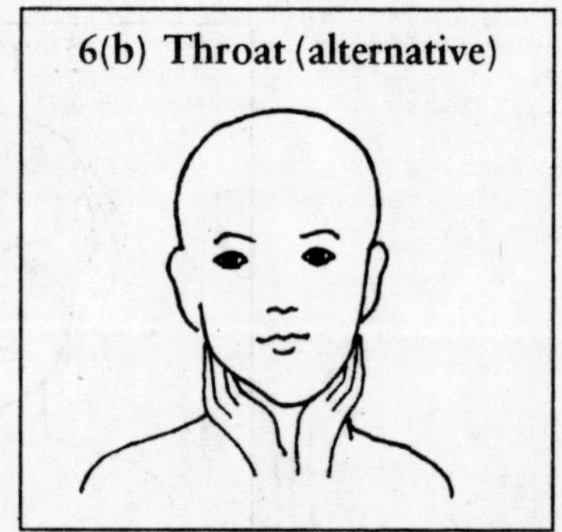
6(b) Throat (alternative)

*Keep thumbs folded in.*

*Note: At throat one hand in front and one hand at the back (not shown in illustration) is also a preferred position.*

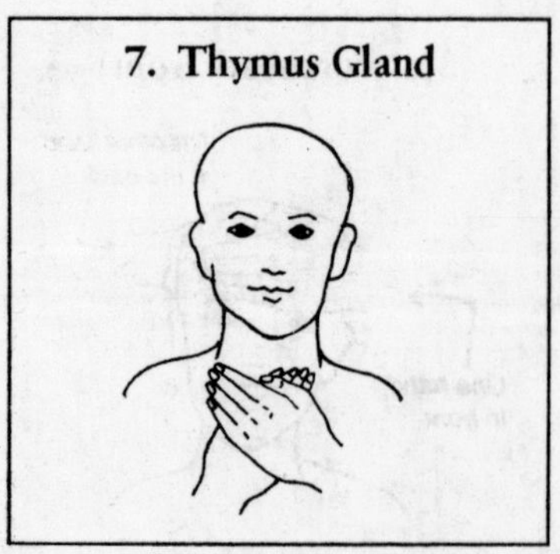
7. Thymus Gland

*Thymus below the collar bone level.*

## The 26/31 Point Positions

### Front Body Positions (continued)

**8(a) Heart—self**
**Centre of chest**

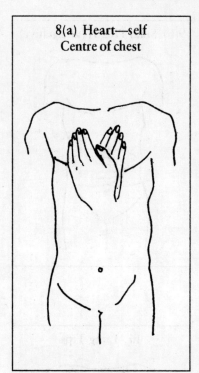

*If Reiki is given to others, especially women, hands may be 2–3 inches away from the body.*

**8(b) Heart—self (alternative)**
**If the hand is pulled/drawn off the central position, allow it to happen.**

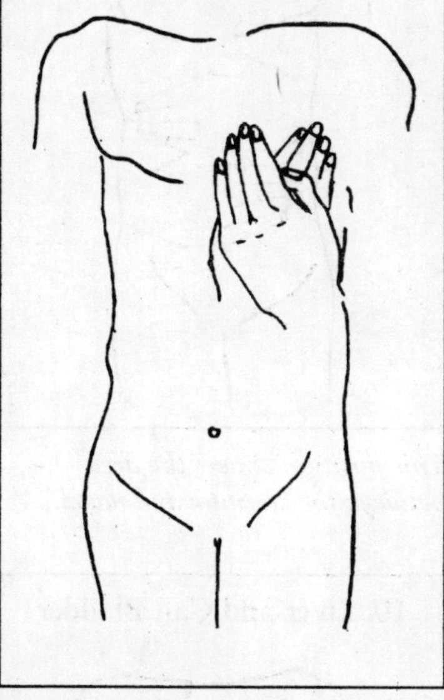

*Right hand should always touch the body at the front heart—that is, the right hand should be under the left hand at the heart point.*

# The 26/31 Point Positions

## Front Body Positions (continued)

**9(a) Solar Plexus**

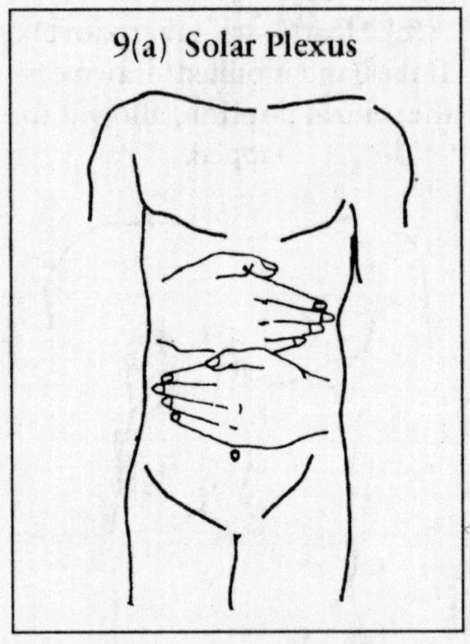

*This position covers the area between the sternum and navel.*

**9(b) Solar Plexus (alternative)**

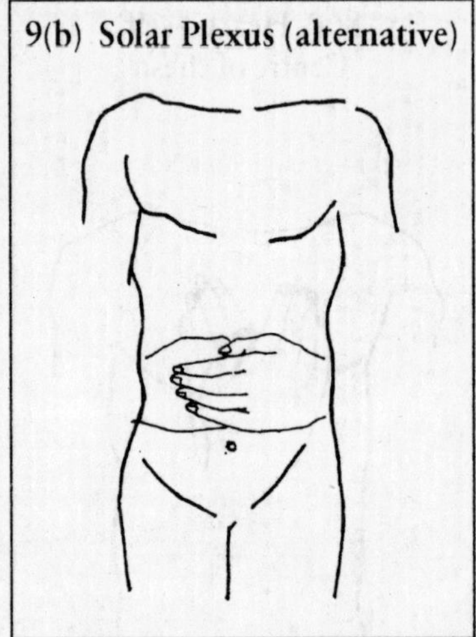

**10. Liver and Gall Bladder**

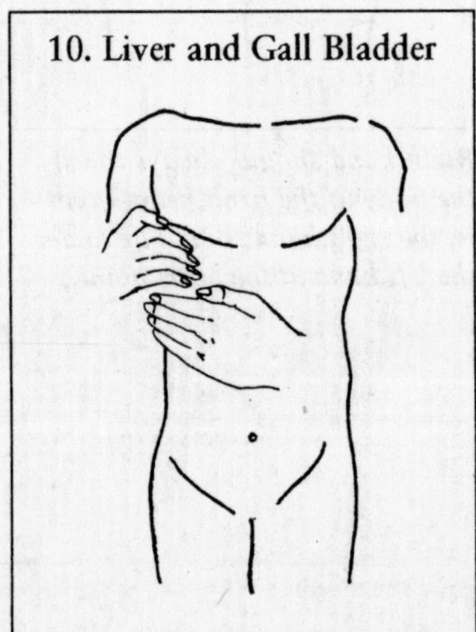

**11. Lung Tips**

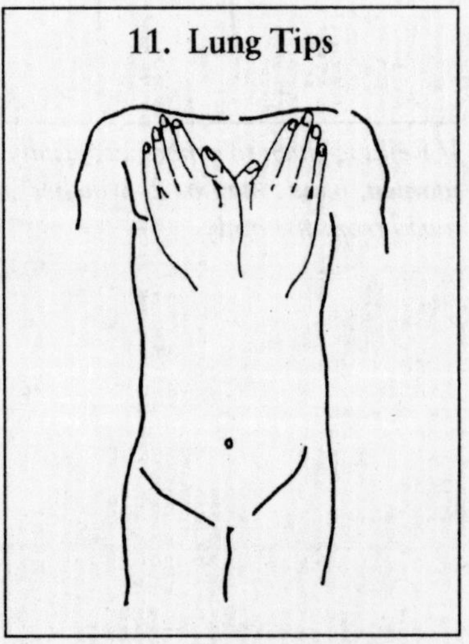

## The 26/31 Point Positions

### Front Body Positions (continued)

12. Spleen and Pancreas

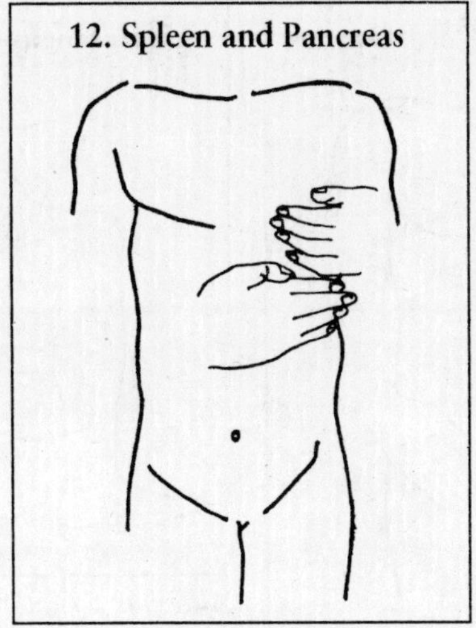

13(a) Hara

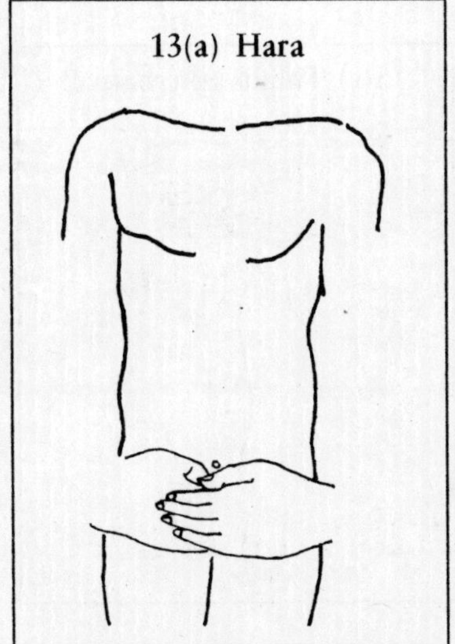

13(b) Hara (Don't)

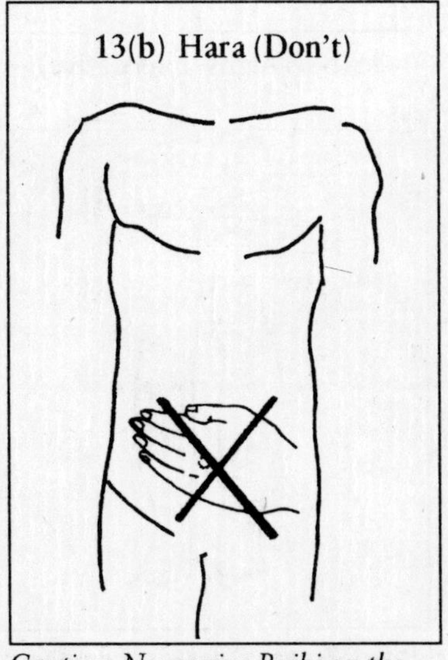

*Caution: Never give Reiki on the navel.*

# The 26/31 Point Positions

## Front Body Positions (continued)

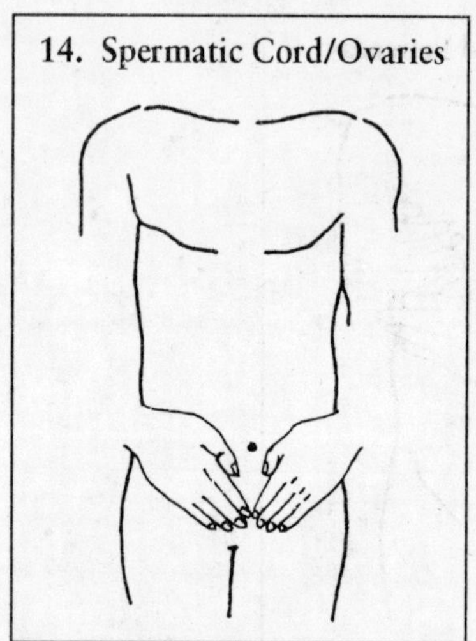

14. Spermatic Cord/Ovaries

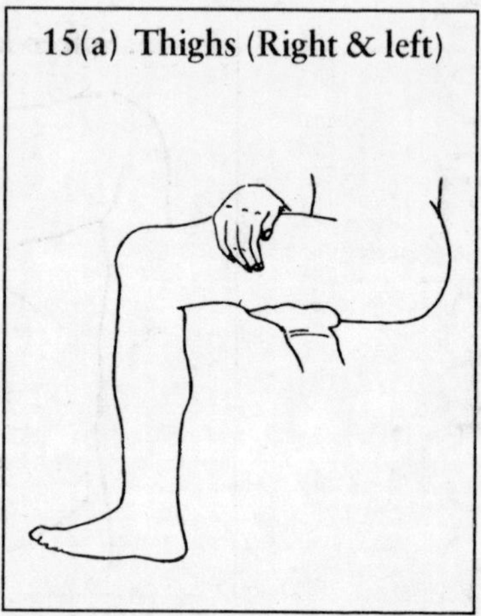

15(a) Thighs (Right & left)

*Alternate position*

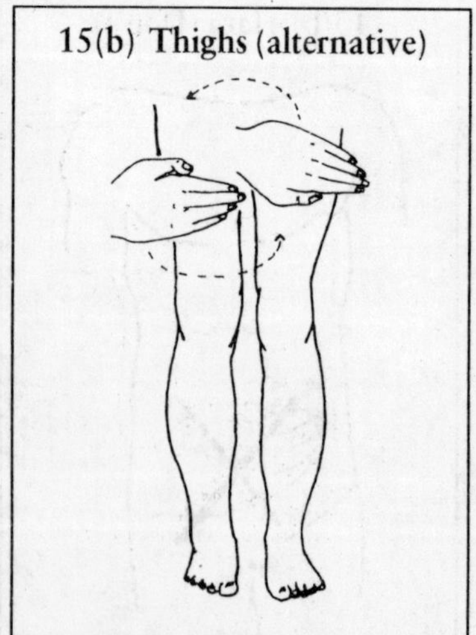

15(b) Thighs (alternative)

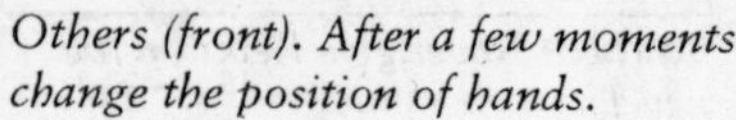

*Others (front). After a few moments change the position of hands.*

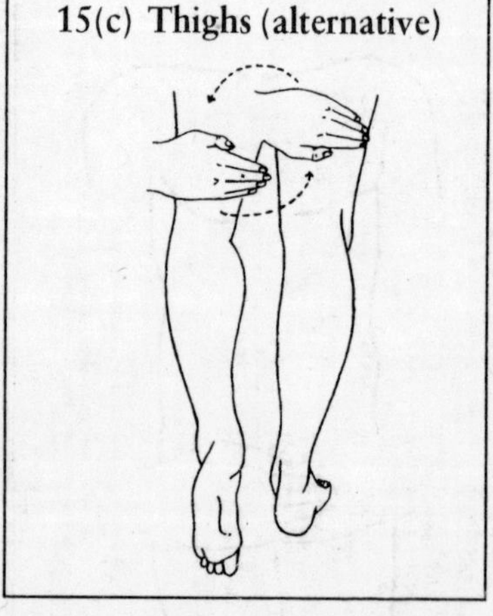

15(c) Thighs (alternative)

*Others (back). After a few moments change the position of hands.*

# The 26/31 Point Positions

## Front Body Positions (continued)

16(a) Knees

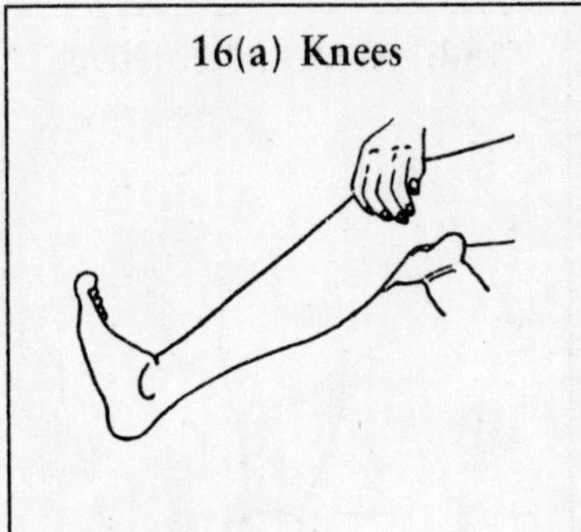

16(b) Knees (alternative)

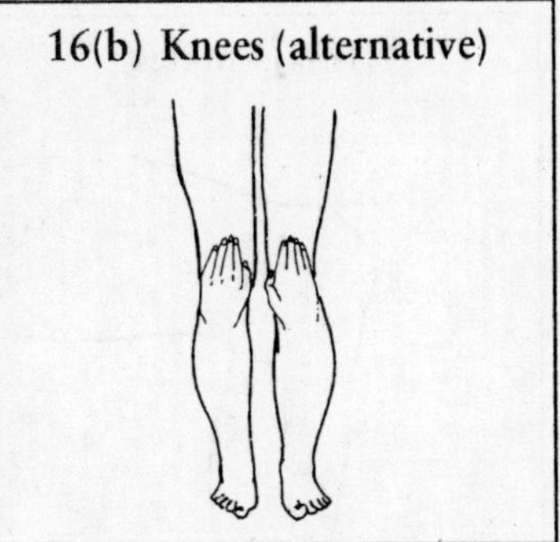

*Top: Knee (self and others)*
*Top right: Knees front (others)*

*Right: Back of Knees (others)*

*Bottom: Calf—using both hannds (self and alternate for others)*

*Bottom right: Calves back (others)*

16(c) Knees (alternative)

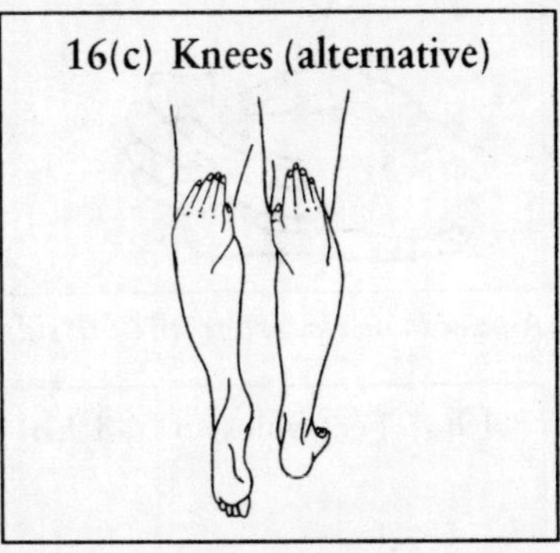

17(a) Calf

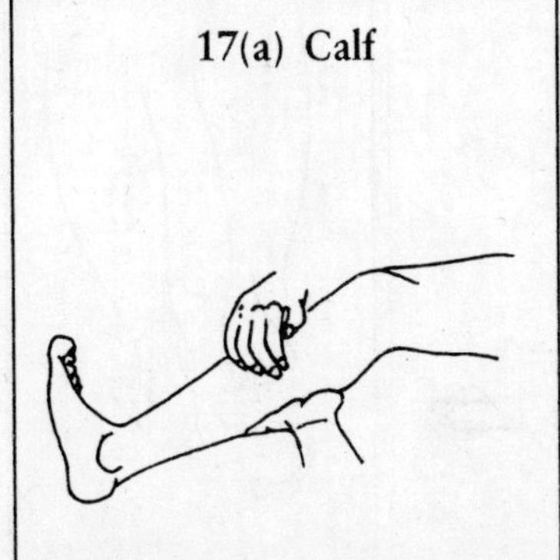

17(b) Calves (alternative)

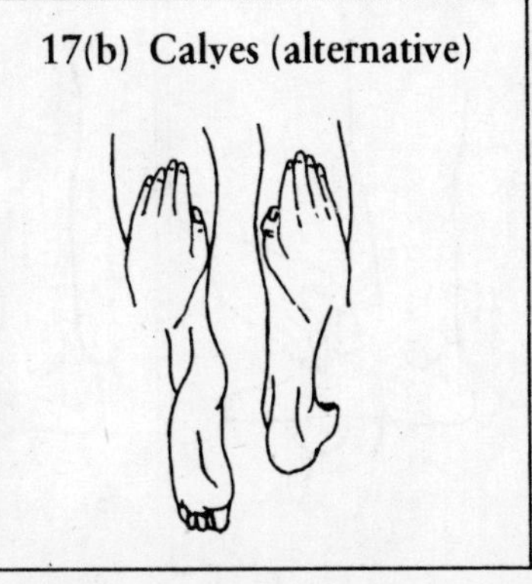

# The 26/31 Point Positions

## Front Body Positions (continued)

18(a) Ankles

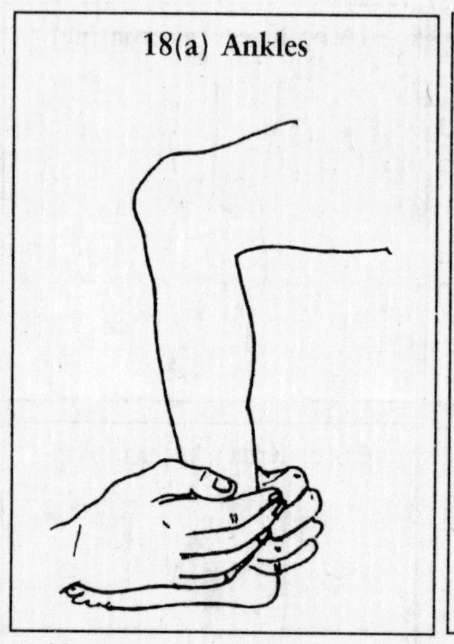

18(b) Ankles (alternative)

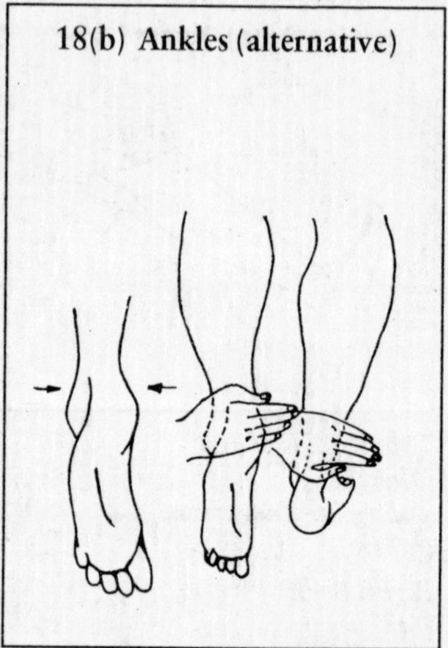

*Ankles to be clasped from both sides.*

19(a) Feet Soles

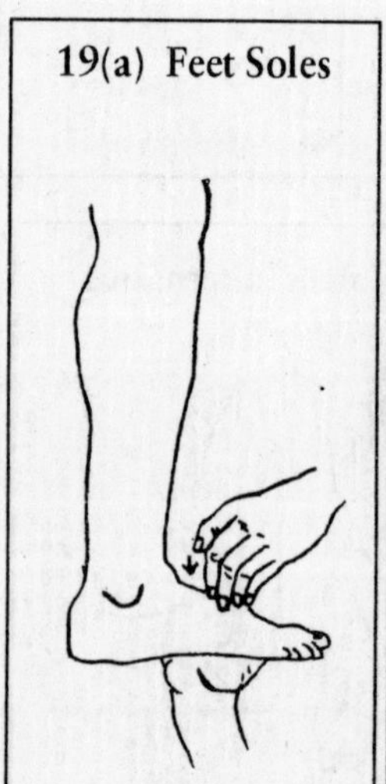

19(b) Feet Soles

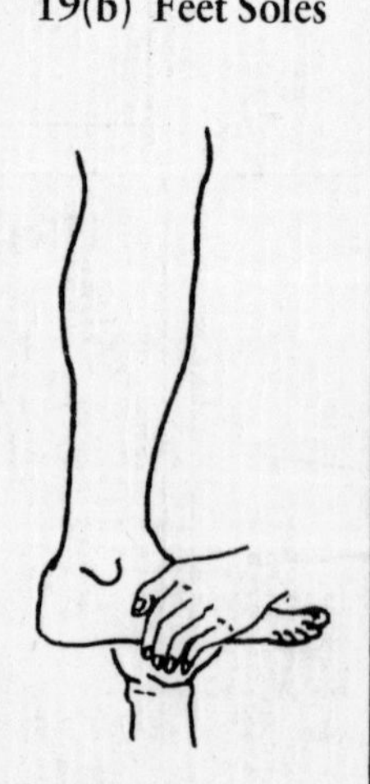

19(c) Feet Soles (alternative)

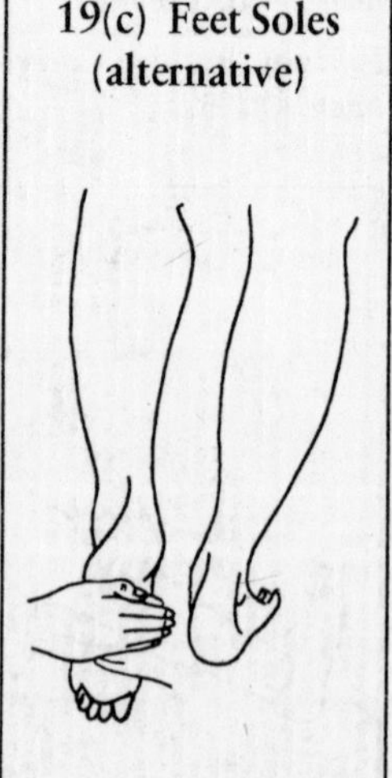

*Self and others*

## The 26/31 Point Positions

### Back Body Positions

**20(a) Shoulders**

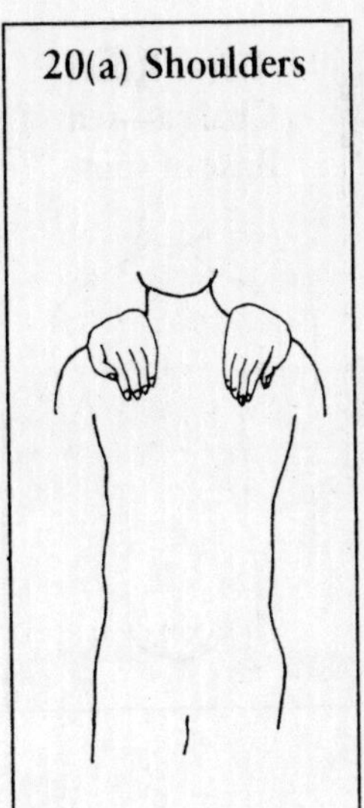

**20(b) Shoulders (alternative)**

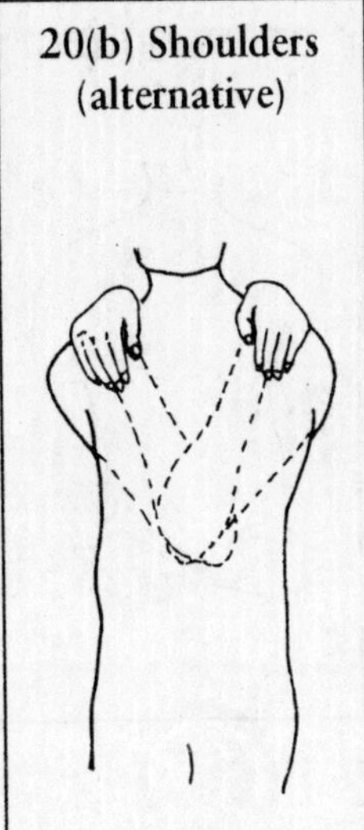

**21. Thymus (back)**

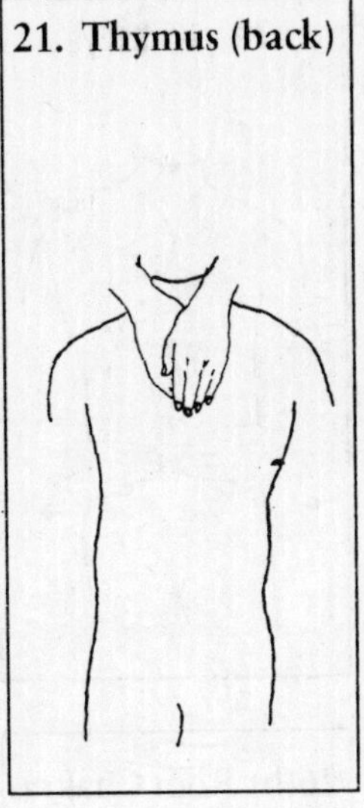

**22. Heart (back)**

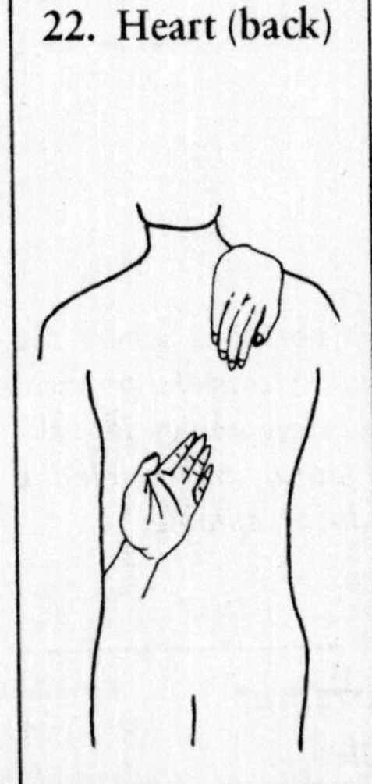

**23(a) Solar Plexus (back)**

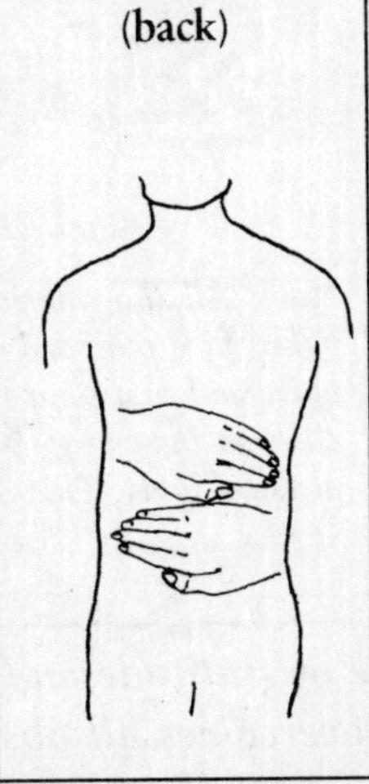

**23(b) Solar Plexus (back) (alternative)**

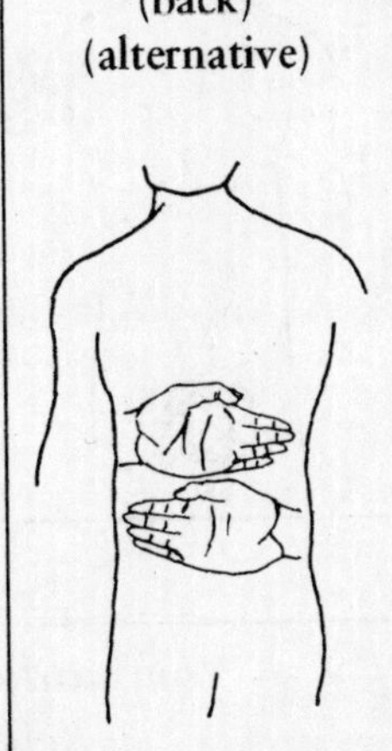

# The 26/31 Point Positions

## Back Body Positions (continued)

24. Kidneys

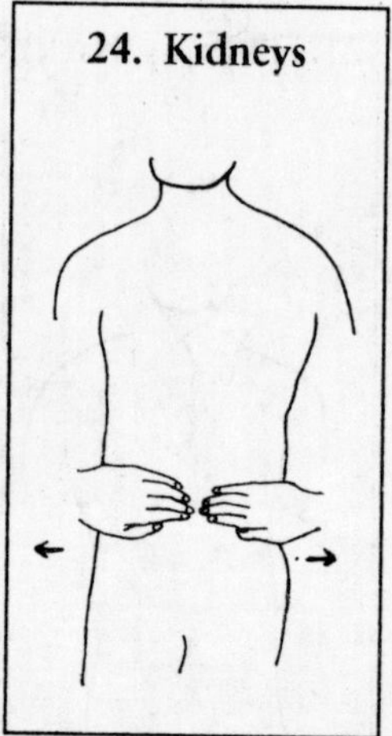

25. Hara(back)

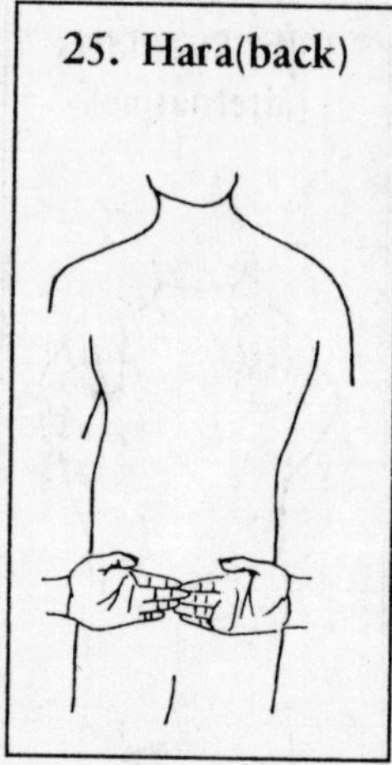

26(a) Root Chakra—self Base of spine

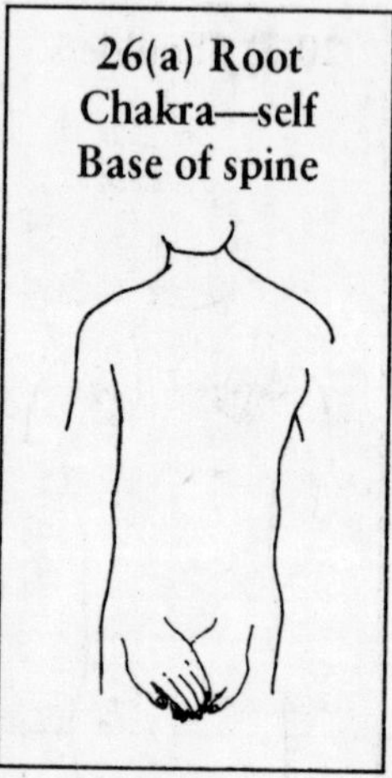

26(b) Root Chakra (alternative)

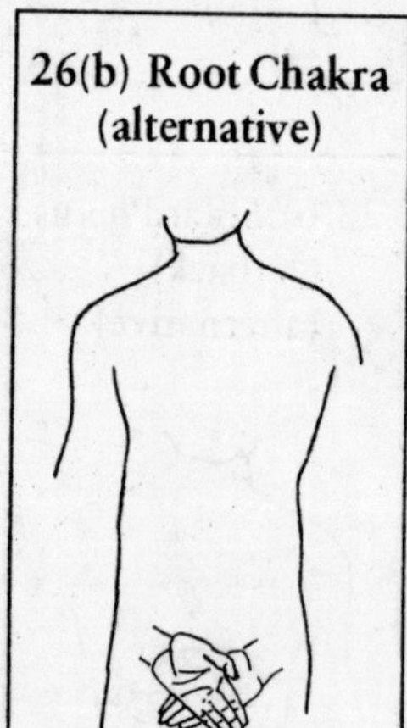

*Note: All the alternative positions where the palms face outward or away from the physical body will first send the healing energy into the chakras and energy body (aura), and then to the physical body. This is quite acceptable.*

***Your attitude of gratitude and surrender to Reiki overcomes all obstacles.***

# 14

# 'Doing Reiki Healing': General Guidelines

## The Basics

Make sure hands are clean and fingers are free of rings.

- Gold absorbs and transmutes negative energy into positive, and where gold rings are worn and healing given on a regular basis, the time lag for transmutation means that negative energy is available to affect you to some degree. Finger-joint pains are a common experience where rings are worn while giving healing on a regular basis. Removing the rings during the healing solves the problem.
- While giving healing to others you cannot 'catch' their infections or diseases.

However, if we are 'sympathetic', vibrating at the healee's emotional frequency, by the law of *Like attracts like,* we are liable to pick up some negative emotional energy (anger, depression, sorrow, etc.) from the healee. Reiki channels hold much less negative energy than others, and a sudden rush of 'sympathy' for the healee will attract some of his negative energy into the Reiki channel's solar plexus chakra. As the Reiki channel's chakras and energy body are much cleaner than the healee's, he is likely to pick up healee's emotional negative energy which will *temporarily* affect him. This is a standard mechanism that operates for all people and has nothing to do with Reiki healing. (In fact, the Reiki flowing in the healer quickly dissolves that negative energy, but he may feel uncomfortable for a while.)

Thus, instead of vibrating at others' negative energy level, Reiki healers may instead radiate loving Reiki energy to the healees through their heart centres. (See *'Sending Healing Across Space and Time'—the Divine Reiki Light, p. 179.*)

Reiki flowing outward is a one-way flow and does not permit negative energies to flow back to the healer.

## 'Feedback'

'Feedback' may be felt as different changes in sensations in your hands—a magnetic pull-push, tingling, warmth-cold, etc. All these indicate positive energy flow.

- *When these sensations start reducing, enough healing has been given at that particular point.*

You may also receive inner guidance, a thought, a 'feeling' that enough healing has been received at that point—all these feedbacks are valid. Learn to work with and trust your intuition more and more in these matters. The more you practise healing yourself and others, the more you will understand this feedback.

- Sometimes you will be guided to move your hand slightly away from, but near the technically correct position—*allow this to happen.* This means the chakra is displaced and you are receiving accurate 'feedback' (response) regarding this condition.

## No 'Feedback'

Quite frequently, Reiki channels receive no *'feedback'* in their hands while healing. At the same time, the *healee* receiving healing may feel sensations of heat or tingling indicating that the energy is flowing. This is different from a 'block' or 'no flow' of Reiki.

The channel is not receiving 'feedback' in the hands because the palm and finger chakras of the healer Reiki channel are not lined up over the physical palm and fingers. As the Reiki channel's self-healing progresses, the hand chakras start lining up, and 'feedback' in hands will start being received.

No 'feedback' in hands is *not* a cause for concern where the Reiki attunements received are genuine and as long as some healees initially feel the energy, or they confirm results.

## 'Blocks', 'No-flow' of Reiki

Sometimes at a particular point during treatment, there may be no sensation of any energy flowing through your hands. A cold/dead feeling may be felt as compared to previously felt warmth/tingling, etc.

This means that there is an *energy block* at that point.

It may take some time before the energy penetrates the block and you start getting positive 'feedback' on energy flow again.

*The blocks can be dissolved* by utilizing *Cleansing Beams* of light as invoked in the white light meditation (Appendix 1), but used differently.

## Block Removal: The Cleansing Beams Method

This technique was observed and developed clairvoyantly by *Sensei* Renoo Nirula and is very effective for removing negative energies, especially of pain and fear.

## The Cleansing Beams

The Cleansing Beams automatically leave ten minutes after appearing.

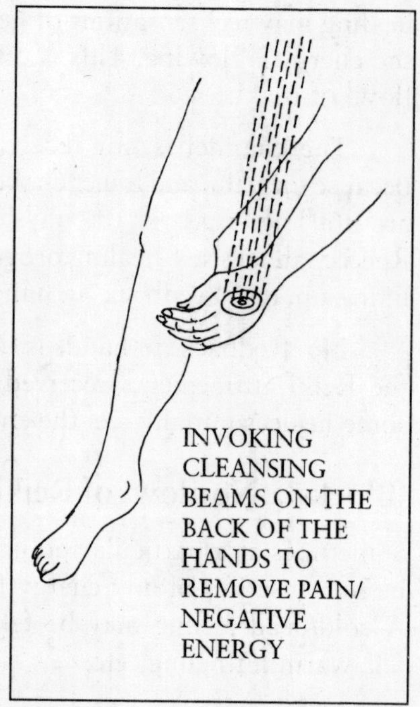
INVOKING CLEANSING BEAMS ON THE BACK OF THE HANDS TO REMOVE PAIN/ NEGATIVE ENERGY

You can programme the time of their appearance for less than that if you like, or, after you feel the block is removed, request the beams, *'Please go back to the source as love and light—thank you'*.

Clairvoyantly seen, at that time you receive Cleansing Beams of light of the appropriate colour at the back of your hands which will actually 'suction up and away' the negative energies. *(Do not specify any colour for the Cleansing Beams)*.

## Invoking the Cleansing Beams

To invoke the Cleansing Beams, while giving Reiki at the point where you experience a block, *mentally state:*

- '*Father-Mother God* (or) *Father-Mother of the Universe,* please send Cleansing Beams of light at the back of my hands which beams send all negativities back to the source as love and light . . . thank you.'
- After the block is removed (30 seconds to a few minutes), thank the beams and Father-Mother of the Universe/Father-Mother God for the healing and request the beams: 'Please go back to the source as love and light, thank you.'

- Alternatively, you may call for the beams and specifying the time-duration they may stay (upto ten minutes), request them in advance to 'Go back to the source as love and light at the end of the specified period, thank you.'

The advantage of doing this is that you can use the beams to remove blocks at more than one point without having to remember to send the beams back after the ten-minute period.

- Therefore, in such a case you would say: 'Father-Mother (of the Universe)/(God), please send me Cleansing Beams of light at the back of my hands which beams send all negativities back to source as love and light, thank you. . . The beams may go back to the source as love and light after ten minutes with thanks and gratitude to the Cleansing Beams and Father-Mother (of the Universe)/(God).'

If you need the beams for more than ten minutes, then send away the current beams within ten minutes (doing Reiki at two or three points) and get fresh ones. Recycle the fresh beams similarly within ten minutes, and so on.

## Pain

*Pain is also an energy block.* The Cleansing Beams method is a very powerful method of removing/relieving pain that is resistant.

## 'Forbidden' Area for Cleansing Beams

The Cleansing Beams may not be used on any frontal chakras or points between the forehead and heart. If there are any blocks experienced on these frontal points, the corresponding area at the *back* may be treated with the Cleansing Beams. Cleansing Beams are usually not required for infants and children. If in doubt, especially for children, avoid using the beams.

## Beams Used on Forbidden Points

If, by mistake, you use the beams on forbidden points, and you remember this later—*at that time mentally request Reiki to rectify and heal this.* Use the Divine Reiki Light procedure detailed in the section *'Sending Healing Across Space and Time' p. 179.*

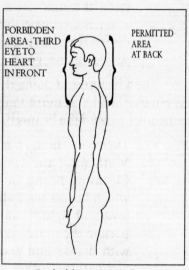

FORBIDDEN AREA - THIRD EYE TO HEART IN FRONT

PERMITTED AREA AT BACK

*Forbidden area in front; Permitted area at back.*

There is no loss or harm because Reiki protection is always there for you and the healee.

However, *when you become aware of some error or mistake on your part, you must do whatever is necessary to rectify it.*

Please do not neglect it out of laziness or feeling, 'Reiki will sort it out, I can relax!'

*Reiki is not our servant!* We must always do our work honestly and such rectification *(even after the event)* is part of this work.

## Beams Invoked Without Time Limits

If you invoke the beams without specifying a time, remember that they will automatically disconnect after about ten minutes.

If you need the beams for a longer time, send the current beams back to the source as love and light before ten minutes have passed and invoke fresh beams.

This is important, as the beams may disconnect while you are under the impression that they are still active.

### Beams 'Forgotten'

If you forget to send the beams back for any reason, *whenever you remember,* formally state that they may go back to the source as love and light with thanks, etc. (*There is no loss or harm.*)

### Beams Not Seen

It is not required that you actually see these beams—the intention is enough and they will appear on your request.

### Healing Chronic Conditions: 21 Healings Cycle

For chronic (long established) conditions such as arthritis, diabetes, heart disease, etc., work on the following pattern:

- Full-body Reiki + Chakra Balancing for three or four consecutive days.

  Thereafter, Full-body Reiki + Chakra Balancing every alternate day, or three times a week, for a total of 21 healing sessions and continue further as needed.
- If you can give 21 days' consecutive healing that is very effective.

Either of the above procedures sets up a healing and cleansing cycle, at the end of which (21 days of actual touch healing which may take place over three weeks or longer) a major shift takes place internally, in the aura body and in the external life situation.

Sometimes the health benefits take time to filter down to the body—be patient.

At the same time, remember that the healee must not be discouraged from taking other therapeutic measures as may be required. Be considerate. Review the healings given. See if you need to rectify something in the treatment at your end.

## Healing Acute Conditions

For acute conditions involving trauma or pain, healing may be given directly to the site of the injury/pain.

If touching the injured/painful part is not feasible, the hands held 3–6 inches (8–15 cm) away from the area will have the same effect as direct touch.

## 'Reiki Didn't Work'

*As an observed fact, Reiki always works.* When you experience 'Reiki didn't work' for a particular situation, you must review the healing. There are a number of reasons why Reiki apparently didn't work in a particular situation.

- The healee's problems are very deep rooted—such conditions take longer to heal. Be patient.
- If you send healing to a person who has not asked for it, the results take longer to appear.
- If the person you send healing to is *unaware* that healing is being sent, the results take longer to appear.

If the person does not want to be healed or resists being healed, the results may not appear at all. This is not uncommon. *We do not force healing where it is not wanted. Do not 'throw' Reiki where there is insufficient respect for the healing.* Exceptions are: your own family members and close associates, because such associations are formed out of deep positive and negative karmic debts to each other. These are best harmonized by sending such persons Reiki at a distance even if the persons do not want Reiki, because the harmonizing of your relationship and interaction with such persons is an essential part of your own self-healing process.

- If sufficient energy exchange is not there, the healee may start becoming offensive internally (refer to details in previous section on 'Attitude of Gratitude').
- If the healee is offensive (critical) towards Reiki channels, the results will not appear, and may instead cause a cleansing reaction in the healee to dissolve his offense.
- An offensive or critical-judgemental attitude in the healee may sometimes be a result of *our own immature dealings* with them, or arising out of *our own false ego.* In such conditions *we must rectify ourselves first,* and avoid giving the other an opportunity to become offensive on our account.
- It may be the current attitude of the healee to be critical or offensive towards Reiki; in such a case there is no need to try and convince the healee about Reiki's merits—*refuse to be drawn into any controversial discussion.* We don't have to prove anything.
- The results of Reiki healing are there for all to see. Acceptance or rejection of Reiki's merits by uninformed persons or *non-practitioners* is of no importance to our healing work and does not affect it adversely.

## Healing Non-acceptors

If you are very determined or desirous of sending healing to a person who is non-accepting , there is no need to be helpless.

As a Reiki channel *you can turn the* 'O' for 'Obstacle' into 'O' for 'Opportunity to Heal' and learn more as to how Reiki can work.

To resistant or non-accepting persons, you can first send healing to *create and manifest* the *intention* that the person *has accepted* being healed and therefore *has accepted* the Reiki healing, and any negative utterances or thoughts by them against healing are automatically recalled and cancelled.

Use the distance healing methods of the Reiki Box and the Divine Reiki Light for manifesting Intentions and Affirmations at the Reiki-1 level. (Reiki-2 and above may empower this further with the mystic symbols.)

Such healing of non-acceptors may require more time before results appear—even weeks and months.

Thus, in practical terms, while sending healing to such persons we may keep this possibility in mind and not invest in great expectations for quick results—although sometimes you will get these! As a Reiki channel in such a situation there is no loss for anyone, only gain.

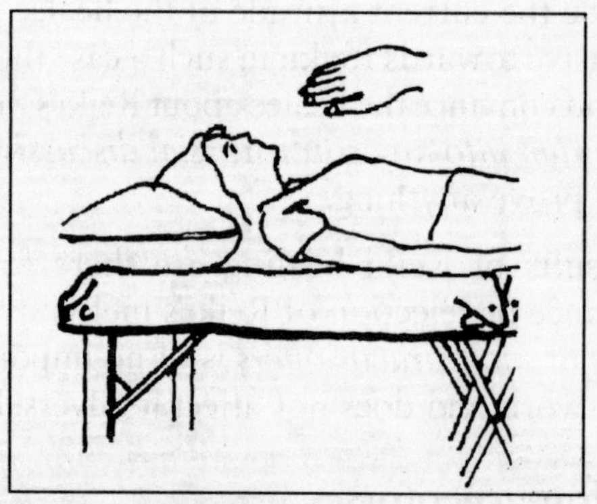

*When giving Reiki to others, especially to sensitive parts like a woman's bosom, the hand should be 2–3 inches away from the body.*

> 'You are never helpless when you have Reiki. Whatever the situation, whatever the trauma or sorrow, you always have Reiki flowing through your hands and your heart—you can always *Reiki it . . . harmonize it* and *heal it*—Whatever It is!'

# 15

# *Emotions and the Body*

As we think, emotions may be generated within us, and as we feel certain emotions, they filter down to the body and affect it. If the emotion is negative, such as arising out of anger, hatred, and so on, then some corresponding biochemicals are released within the body and start to affect it according to the nature of the emotion-thought. These biochemicals convey the quality of that particular emotion to the body, and if the emotion is of a 'negative' nature, then that quality is embodied in those biochemicals and conveyed to various body parts. These elements accumulate in our bodies if not digested and if not eliminated or discharged.

*It is this accumulation, non-elimination of toxic biochemicals originating from unhappy negative emotions-thoughts that then leads to disease.*

On the other hand, if we have positive thoughts and emotions, the physical body responds by releasing chemical analogues of such feelings leading to a feeling of 'well-ness' within our bodies. This is the internal communication system of the various subtle emotional-mental-spiritual bodies to the gross physical body.

'Positive thinking' is a mechanism of one of the subtle bodies—the *manomaya kosh* or mental sheath. As we shall explore and find out, 'positive thinking' is not *Reiki,* although it is an important mechanism in the scheme of how health and disease manifest. Healing with Reiki is a matter of being *authorized and empowered with unconditional loving healing energy* which overcomes all obstacles, and is not dependent on positive thinking.

A fundamental precept of ayurveda is: *Indigestion is the mother of all diseases.* This means and includes all that we are unable to digest mentally, emotionally, physically. According to ayurveda, it is in our subtle emotional-mental bodily aura that this mechanism is first generated as *ama,* or 'subtle disease substance'. If it is neither digested nor eliminated, the end-result is discomfort, 'disease', that leads to functional changes in our well-being, and finally when pathological tissue changes take place there is 'diagnosed disease'.

On the physical level this is exemplified by overeating which causes indigestion and its subsequent consequences.

Common examples of subtle indigestion are migraine (headaches) accompanied by nausea, which are seen to originate from emotional indigestion, while fear, fright and anxiety may cause sudden passing of urine or stool.

Long-term fear may cause weakness at the knees and ultimately chronic pain, inflammation, and lack of mobility—the equivalent of being rooted to the spot, unable to move by fear. This condition is then diagnosed as arthritis or rheumatism. Prolonged emotional and mental indigestion (chronic stress) can create many serious conditions such as ulcers, gall-bladder stones and related pancreatitis, coronary artery disease.

Thus, we can understand by personal practical experience that undigested emotions-thoughts, blockages in our emotions-thoughts, are all 'stored' in certain organs or systems of the body, in certain body parts. This is true regardless of our cultural orientations, sex or age. It is a universal reality.

In a practical sense, while trying to understand our ailments, it is useful to remember that:

1. The bodily part affected is directly related to an emotional state of the individual and his life condition.
2. All right-sided complaints have to do with the individual's own self, own family (parents, husband-wife, children, brothers-sisters, uncles-aunts), and own personal goals, objectives, etc.
3. Left-sided complaints have to do with the rest of the world—the 'others'.

To a Reiki channel who has healing experience, every ailment tells a story as to where the person is in his life. This is so because the ailment will reflect the individual's inner emotional condition, his inner distress, his inner attitudes that need to be healed.

In continuing exploration of this mechanism, we find that 'accidents' are also not a casual thing: they are the sharply delivered results of our inner condition. Where a particular body part is involved, what that part represents in our life is *already* traumatized—*before* the physical takes place.

*The prior subtle emotional background always appears first. If this is corrected and healed, then the previously due material consequence cannot take place as the situation has already changed with the healing.*

The purpose of the karmic result due has already been served—in other words our past karma and destiny have been healed, harmonized, in this way.

Where the purpose of karmic results-reactions are served, then there is no need for them to be activated. So-called 'negative' (painful and undesirable) karmic results are meant to forcefully teach us those lessons we do not readily learn and which are essential for our inner self-development. Sometimes one learns just by seeing another's example, and sometimes one needs repeated personal experience of painful reactions in order to learn. With Reiki, very significant, radical neutralization and harmonization of karma takes place. Such is the experiencc of all our Reiki channels who do their self-healing with commitment.

This is the secret of how by healing one's own body and self, one can heal one's whole life, profession and bank balance!

*Karma* or our actions cause certain effects in our lives. The word karma simply means 'action, activity, to do'. *And it is our own actions that cause certain results—no one else is responsible.* These actions can be healed and harmonized by Reiki only because the universal life force energy *actually empowers us* to heal, harmonize, make whole and complete sufficiently, *all material conditions*. This specific empowerment is not seen elsewhere in other systems.

Sometimes we may be confused on seeing apparently 'causeless' diseases—the individual didn't apparently 'do' anything to cause his problem. Where there is no apparent cause for disease in terms of attitudinal or emotional position, or where it is very mildly present—the disease or disorder must be understood as being *deeply karmic* in nature, requiring persistent healing.

We need to understand that the whole universe is running on a law of cause and effect. As we act, so do we get a particular result. And at some point the individual occupying this current bodily vehicle created current karma, or his 'destiny', including the disease, the internal block.

How does this happen? This is further dealt with in the explanation and expansion of the five principles of Reiki at the end of this book, and in the section entitled 'Universal Life and Emotional Energy Activity Principles'.

However, we may consider here the evidence for past lives, continuing lives and karmic reactions.

When we were in the womb, or newly born and then nine or ten years old, then thirty and so on—by comparing bodies we would not be able to say with certainity that the bodies belong to the same individual. And yet, the individual *knows* that he was that same person at age five, twenty or thirty or sixty—even though the bodily form has changed radically; and modern medical science tells us that every cell of the body changes within seven years cyclically. Thus, every seven years, we have a 'new' physical body although it appears to be the 'same' body that is changing.

Although the body *is* changing, our consciousness, our awareness of ourself as to who we are remains essentially the same—we do not claim that at age twenty we are not the same person or individual we were at age ten, although we would have matured, both physically and mentally. The sense of 'who I am' remains through all the changes—the essential 'I-ness' or 'I-consciousness' remains: *I know I am essentially the same person, the same being I was ten years ago or twenty or thirty years ago.*

I do not speak and behave as though I am a completely different personality—and if I do, then this may be diagnosable as a multiple personality disorder or a condition of schizophrenia requiring medical attention. Thus, even though I undergo changes, there is an essential part of me *that does not change but travels* as it were in these different bodies. This is the personal experience of each one of us.

This is evidence that we, the essential, unchanging part of ourselves we call 'me' or 'I' is travelling in changing bodies all the time. There is no time that we do *not* move in different and changing bodies starting from the time we are the size of a pea in the womb until we leave our body finally when it is no longer able to be of service.

In the world around us, there is no evidence and it is no one's experience that we do *not* travel in changing or different bodies. Therefore, it is perfectly reasonable, logical, rational to accept the fact that when the body's functions cease, the essential unchanging part of me will once again move to another body, changing or transferring to a body which can be a suitable vehicle for the essential, unchanging 'me'.

Clairvoyantly seen, the essential unchanging, spiritual (non-material) elemental part of ourselves changes bodies like we change clothes, but clothes we are very attached to! Because we have identified ourselves with our bodies and its expansions and extensions, we have a problem with so-called 'death' which is only a major change of bodies, while the constant minor changing of the body is accepted as the 'aging' process.

As we do our Reiki self-healing and connect more and more with this, our true, essential unchanging self, we become aware by direct experience of its (and our own) true qualities, the first of which is our essential unchanging or immortal and deathless nature. This realization is direct perception of Truth, and the first stage of self-realization—of knowing who we really are.

All this is available easily with Reiki at the Reiki-1 level. Sometimes we take a long while realizing it because it is outside our previous experience and we have no reference within to compare it with. It is new, and even though difficult to identify, it is something we like because connecting with that state makes us feel joyous and peaceful.

Children are very connected to Reiki energies and often connect with this. It is adults who can't really understand it too well. We recall a long-ago childhood poem that expresses this and other commonly shared but inexplicable feelings beautifully:

*I feel a feel, a funny feel,*
*a funny feel feel I*
*And if you feel the feel I feel—*
*You'll feel the same as I.*

# 16

# The Human Body and its Life Energy Field

The different subtle energy bodies taken together form the life energy field (also known as the 'aura') that functions through the physical body. Each layer of the aura originates at each of the indicated chakras (energy spinning wheels or vortexes). When the chakra spins it generates a colour which is specific to that chakra in a state of good health. The following illustration shows how these layers are placed.

Generally, the total aura extends around the physical body from a few centimeters to a few inches. Spiritually developed persons have much larger auras. The larger the aura, the healthier the person, his life full of positive abundant energies.

Reiki channels have very large auras.

In a healthy, energy-clean environment, the aura has a tendency to expand and grow larger. We observed that one of our Reiki-3As in Rajpur, Dehradun, had an aura that extended beyond Roorkee—a linear distance of about 60 kilometres, giving his aura a diameter of 120 kilometres.

While the 'normal' size of the seven major chakras may vary from between about 3 and 5 inches in diameter (7.5 cm–

12.5 cm), the root chakra of one of our Reiki-3As would generally be as large as 15–16 inches (38–40 cm) in diameter. The largeness of the root chakra indicates not only material opulence but spiritual opulence as well, while the crown chakra represents pure spiritual consciousness, enlightenment.

Reiki channels have correspondingly large crown chakras, about 15–16 inches (38–40 cm) in diameter for a Reiki-3A, with an *antahkaran* (pillar of light) being about 3.5 inches (8 cm) in diameter.

We have observed that spiritually advanced persons following religious methodologies develop an *antahkaran* of between a quarter of an inch (6 mm) to less than half an inch (12 mm) in diameter, and an aura that may be 3 or 4 kilometres in diameter. Very advanced religionists may have auras 6 or 7 kilometres in diameter.

**Key to the Aura Bodies**

| Seven Auras (or Aura Bodies) Connected to the Seven Chakras | |
|---|---|
| 1. Root Chakra | Karmic, spiritual, material body, past memory |
| 2. Hara Chakra | Mental, self-image, false ego body |
| 3. Solar Plexus | Physical health body |
| 4. Heart Chakra | Emotional body |
| 5. Throat Chakra | Astral (communication) body |
| 6. Third Eye (Ajna) Chakra | Divine astral wisdom body |
| 7. Crown Chakra | Divine higher self body |

## The Seven Major Chakras—Energy Centres

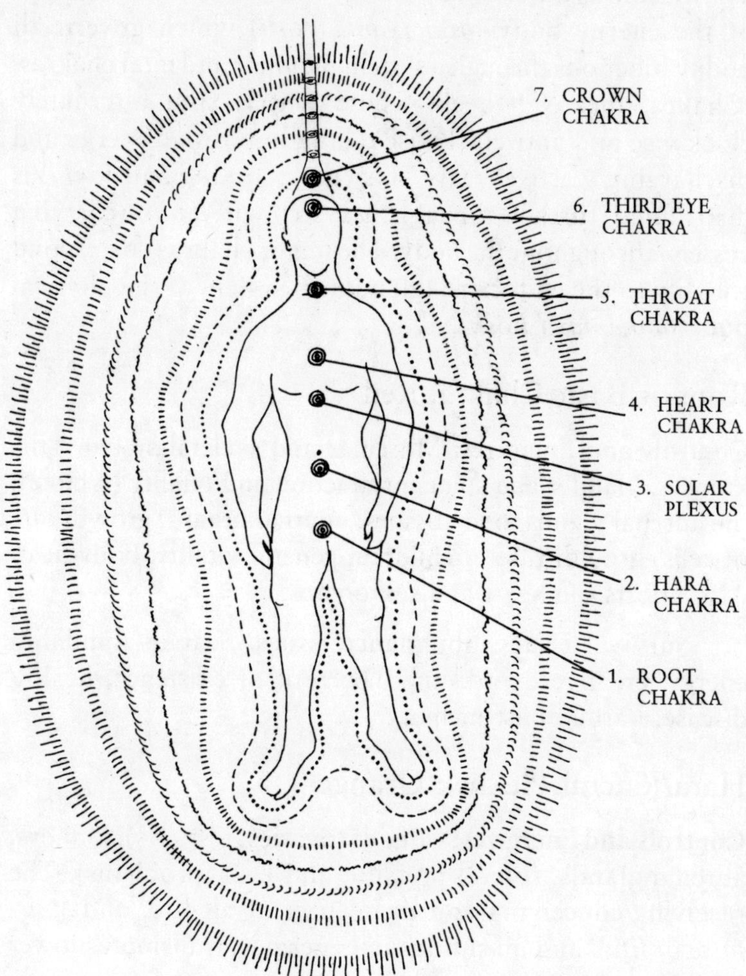


*THE AURA*
THE SEVEN LAYERS OF THE AURA
AND LOCATION OF PRINCIPAL CHAKRAS

## The Seven Major Chakras

These chakras are the main energy accumulators and pumps of the energy body (*pranayama kosh*) which govern all bodily functions through a system of minor and mini chakras. 'Chakra' means 'wheel'. These wheels spin alternately clockwise and anti-clockwise taking in positive energy and discharging waste energy. This energy (*prana* and *Reiki*) is distributed further through a system of *nadis* (carrying vessels) throughout the body. The major chakras correspond roughly to the endocrine (glandular) system of the physical body (*annamaya kosh*).

## Root or Basic Chakra: Red

**Controls and Energizes:** Muscular and skeletal systems, the kidneys, bladder and spine, production and quality of blood, the adrenal glands, body tissues, internal organs, growth rate of cells, growth rate of children, general vitality, body heat. Also affects the heart and sex organs.

Survival issues, abundance issues. Seat of kundalini energy, creative expression. The root of existence, health/ disease, karma, past memory.

## Hara/(Sacral Plexus): Orange

**Controls and Energizes:** Gonads (ovaries, testicles), kidneys, adrenal glands, (blood pressure and back problems). The receiving/conceiving and protection of all life, and '*purpose of life*', and all subtle vital energies; transmutes lower energies.

*Power Centre*: Raises kundalini; transmits vital prana throughout body via spleen chakra, back hara chakra.

We can 'live with ourselves' in hara.

## Solar Plexus Chakra: Yellow

**Controls and Energizes:** Diaphragm, liver, pancreas, stomach; large and small intestines to a great degree, and to some degree the adrenal glands, heart, lungs and other parts of the body.

*Power and Wisdom:* Centre for positive and negative lower emotions such as ambition, courage, aggressiveness, anger, hatred, envy, greed, violence, cruelty, etc.

We *draw feelings* from the solar plexus and *feel* at the heart.

## Heart Chakra: Bright Light Green

**Controls and Energizes:** The heart, lungs, liver and circulatory system, the thymus gland, and the immune system. Seat of the soul/spiritual essence/being.

*Heart Chakra*: Love and compassion. The centre of higher and refined emotions; directly affected by imbalance in the solar plexus chakra.

End receiving point of Divine Reiki energy and distributor of this to arms and hands.

## Throat Chakra: Light Blue

**Controls and Energizes:** The throat, voice box (larynx), air tube (trachea), thyroid and parathyroid glands, lymphatic system. Communication and self-expression.

Also affects the sex chakra. The centre for the lower or concrete mind, lower mental faculty and also the centre for higher creativity.

## Ajna (Third-eye) Chakra: Indigo-Violet

**Controls and Energizes:** The pituitary and hypothalamus glands; autonomic nervous system. Master control chakra for all major chakras and the endocrine system, nervous system (via forehead chakra) and whole body.

## Crown Chakra: Dark Violet-Gold

**Controls and Energizes:** The pineal gland, the upper brain and right eye.

Centre for higher cosmic, universal spiritual consciousness. The entry point for Divine energy, Reiki, via the *antahkaran,* the 'pillar of light' connecting us to our spiritual source.

Gives direct perception of who we are, self-realization—connecting us with our spiritual self.

# 17

# *Forgiveness*

If I hold myself guilty and punishable and therefore not to be forgiven and not to be loved, then equally, I can neither forgive nor love another.

I can only give out what I have within. If I hate and despise myself, then equally must I hate and despise my neighbour, the 'other'.

'Foregoing' or 'giving up' judging, apportioning blame-responsibility on the other for what I feel, is forgiving.

And what is it that we 'give up' or lose by not being judgemental of another? We lose the pain and hurt that is thus far retained within when we hold another responsible for our inner emotional suffering.

Deal with the situation without 'judging', judgementalism.

So *first let go of judging-blaming the others, the 'other' parts of yourself. 'Love thy neighbour as thyself' is only possible if you first love those neighbours closest to you, those parts of yourself which you don't like, which you have judged, condemned and hold separate from what you view 'yourself' as. So let go of judgementalism.*

And in this letting go, this foregoing of judgement, in forgiving, experience a major freedom, a major cleansing healing.

## INTELLECT, TECHNIQUES AND SPONTANEOUS HEALING

'We find many people on the intellectual platform asking analytical questions about Reiki healing. And we answer these at their level and try and take them beyond mere techniques.'

'Technique may be required when we are not working fully from the heart centre and this is the "method" system of healing. It has a certain definiteness which is comforting to the intellect used to method, analysis.'

'But when love flows from the heart freely, when the desire is that the universe be healed—*it is so* much more powerfull than any method.'

'Do not think that we are technicians just because we are teaching you technique and method. Because the Master is teaching you 'abc' right now it does not mean that he knows only 'abc'.'

'When we clairvoyantly view the situation and say to the students, "The Master is sending healing which is why you felt such-and-such and the following thought came in your mind....," the Fourth Grandmaster is not using any technique or method. This is happening naturally in his presence by the love flowing from his heart.'

'And the same happens naturally with all purified Reiki channels as well.'

—*Renoo Nirula*

18

# Body Parts, Disease, Emotions

Parts of the body and the emotions/attitudes accumulated therein cause disorders as listed. While giving Reiki healing, allow your 'feedback' to guide you. Often the disorder requires other chakras to be healed deeply.

| Body Part | Disease + Emotions |
|---|---|
| **1. Nose:** Related to heart. Sense of smell, sexual response, self-recognition. | **Sinusitis, Deviated Septum:** Unsure as to what option should be taken professionally, career-wise or occupationally; or unsure of personal identity. |
| **2. Mouth:** Survival issues. Capacity to take in new ideas/ concepts. | **Cavities in Teeth:** New ideas/ concepts are hard to take in, become 'survival issues' openly if old concepts and belief systems are 'threatened'. |
| | **Calculi in Salivary Glands:** New ideas, concepts are hard to digest, but individual does not openly challenge them. |
| **3. Forehead (third eye, occipital lobes, temples):** Mental, | **All Nerve and Nervous Disorders** (also solar plexus for im- |

| Body Part | Disease + Emotions |
|---|---|
| intellectual expression, nervous system; will-power, wisdom, intuition, mystic powers. | mediate relief of an acute condition of fear, anger, upset, etc.), **sinusitis** (third eye chakra). **Chronic Vertigo:** Lack of discrimination/balance (third eye, temples). (Compare also under: 'Ears', 'Ankle'—colour blindness) **Migraine (headache):** From emotional indigestion—heal the liver. |
| 4. **Neck:** The mental and the emotional come together. Withheld feelings give stiffness here. | **Cervical Spondylosis:** Inability to express what one feels due to conflict between the intellect and heart. (Cervical 5, 6, 7 vertebrae, corresponding to throat chakra.) |
| 5. **Face:** Expression of our personality and how we face the world. | **Trigeminal Neuralgia:** Inability to face the world due to damage of our self-image, self-worth. (Also Reiki heart-and-hara to draw up and *heal* the emotion and thinking: right hand on heart, left hand on hara.) |
| 6. **Eyes:** How we view the world —instant 'like and dislike'; window of soul. | **Colour Blindness:** Lack of dicrimination/balance (Reiki the ankles, particularly effective for colour-blind people.) **Cataracts:** Does not like what he sees in the world. **Degenerative Retinopathy, Retinal Haemorrhage:** Does not like what is seen in his personal |

| Body Part | Disease + Emotions |
|---|---|
| | life; or does not like his view of himself. **Glaucoma:** Inability to weep, unshed tears. |
| **7. Eyebrows:** Emotional expression, third-eye intuitive centre. | |
| **8. Ears:** Capacity to hear and accept the heard. | **Deafness:** Dislikes what is heard. **Vertigo:** Ears and third eye are secondary areas after ankles—primary area if vertigo is caused by mental-emotional trauma due to hearing unpleasant things. **Insomnia:** Coming from overactive thinking, mental activity (which is subtle speech). |
| **9. Jaws:** Emotional and verbal communication. Fear of expressing ourselves. Survival issues. | |
| **10. Arms and Hands:** Extensions of the heart centre. Express love, emotion; *giving and receiving*. Creativity. | **Left hand** = Receiving/taking hand (negative energy taker/transmuter); **Right hand** = Giving hand (positive energy taker/giver/generator). **Paralysis of Arms/Hands:** Extreme hopelessness and helplessness. (Heal *back heart* chakra, *thymus* front and back, *root*. Also review other areas.) |

| Body Part | Disease + Emotions |
|---|---|
| **11. Chest:** Relationship issues. *Power centre for women.* | **Female Tumors of the Breast:** Blockage or trauma to *women's purpose of life,* of the outflow of loving energy. |
| **12. Heart:** Love. Seat of the soul, spiritual being. | **Angina, Ischaemia:** Functional shortage/lack of loving energy at back heart chakra. **Coronary Artery Disease:** Blockage in the flow of love—inability to receive/accept love (Back heart chakra is affected.) **Heart Attack:** Inability to receive/accept love has reached a severely settled traumatic stage. In such a condition, giving Reiki at the *back heart chakra* with the right hand and at *solar plexus* with the left, can be a life-saving procedure and facilitates extremely good recovery. |

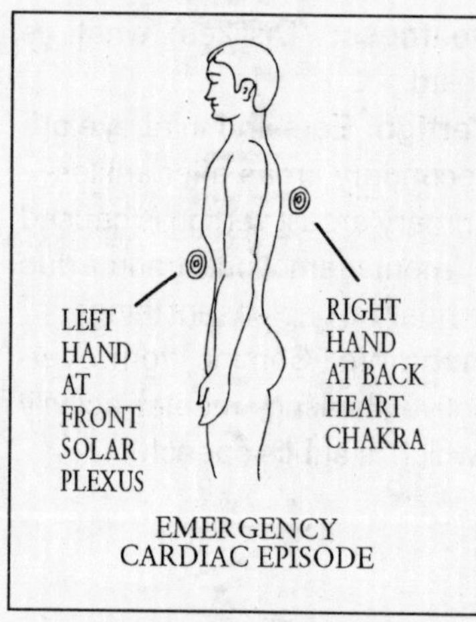

EMERGENCY CARDIAC EPISODE

| Body Part | Disease + Emotions |
|---|---|
| **13. Solar Plexus:** *Power and control issues,* practical wisdom. Immediately experienced emotions of fear, hatred, anger, jealousy, envy, etc. *Also:* courage, and perseverance. (If unbalanced = foolhardy, stubborn.) | **Digestive disorders** |

The *solar plexus* is always involved for *all digestive disorders:* mental-emotional-physical, and all *acute problems including* fever, infections (which need Reiki at *liver, root chakra,* and *affected area).*

| Body Part | Disease + Emotions |
|---|---|
| 14. Abdomen/*Hara:* Seat of deepest emotions, hurt feelings/thinking. *Power centre for men.* | **Hernia, Uterine–Ovarian Disorders; Prostate Disorder; Self-blame, Guilt** ('can't live with myself'). Trauma to the individual's 'purpose of life'. *Unfulfilled/traumatized purposes and desires.* **Very important area for healing.** |
| 15. Liver: Digestion and transmutation of lower emotions to higher. *Emotional indigestion at all levels.* | **Pimples (Acne)**: Dislike/disgust at one's body/bodily parts, processes or changes taking place in body, as in puberty—(**Liver + Hara**). |
| | **Rashes, 'Allergies', Urticaria:** Inability to digest emotions—all arising from the **liver** (and solar plexus). |
| **FEVERS:** *always* involve **liver, solar plexus** and **root chakra.** (Sometimes **spleen**). Many fevers also come from *fear* at the **knees.** | **Gall-stones/pancreatitis:** Undigested emotion/deep hurt unforgiven, solidifies as *gall stones; + anger* = pancreatitis. |
| 16. Spleen and Pancreas: Anger, helplessness. | Spleen is seen to be a part of the digestive system along with the liver, gall-bladder, solar plexus, pancreas chakras. **Blood disorders**. |
| 17. Genitals: Survival and root chakra issues. *Fear of life, existence.* | **Impotence, Sterility:** Purpose of life is deeply traumatized. (Also heal: Hara, kidneys.) |

| Body Part | Disease + Emotions |
|---|---|
| 18. Thighs: Personal strength and trust in one's own abilities. Self-confidence. | **Depression:** Due to, or causing lack of ability to work because of lack of self-confidence. (Also heal solar plexus, back heart, *hara*). |
| 19. Knees: Fear of death. Fear of death of one's ego or own self/consciousness; fear of change/moving ahead. *Personal responsibility issues.* | **Arthritic/Rheumatic Knees:** Fears/anxieties. |
| | ACUTE PAIN or continuing pain anywhere in the body is aggravated or caused by *Fear/Anxiety*. REIKI the *knees* in such cases. DO NOT express 'sympathy' energy or 'Sorrow' as these emotions *sharpen and increase the individuals' perception of his pain!* ('Like attracts like') **Instead:** Request Reiki to open the person's back heart chakra (or send the Divine Reiki Light/Reiki balls, pp. 183/52). |
| 20. Calf: *As for knees and self-control issues.* Addictions/attachments. Fear of change, moving ahead. | **Cramps, Rigidity, Stiffness of Calves:** Does not like or adjust to natural changes taking place in life (and body)—as |

| Body Part | Disease + Emotions |
|---|---|
| | in pregnancy. *Resistance* to moving forward to new condition/ states in life. *Attachment* to the old. Also: *Self-control issues* as in habits, addictions, temper etc., and ***over***-control. |
| **Lower leg:** Fear of action. Capacity for moving towards goals. | **Paralysis of Legs:** Extreme hopelessness and helplessness. *(Heart, Hara and Root chakras would also need healing.)* |
| **21. Ankles:** Balance, discrimination in life activities. | **Ankle injury:** lack of discrimination/balance in activities *(colour-blindness).* |
| **22. Feet:** Connecting with and reaching one's goals. *Fear of* ***completion*** *of activities. Procrastination, laziness.* | **Foot injury:** inability or resistance in moving forward towards goals, while life events overwhelmingly indicate movement is essential. |
| **23. Shoulders:** Responsibility area. | **Cervical Ribs, Shoulder Pains:** Carrying assumed burdens and responsibilities not rightfully one's own. |
| **24. Upper Back** *(Thymus)*: Storehouse of unconscious emotions and tensions. *Anger.* | **Upper Back Disorders:** Results of: stored anger, frustration and helplessness. |
| **25. Lower Back:** *(back hara).* Storage of unresolved emo- | **'Slipped (Herniated) Spinal Disk; (Lumbar) Spondylosis:** |

| Body Part | **Disease + Emotions** |
|---|---|
| tions. *Relationship issues.* (Lumbar 4, 5, 6 vertebrae, and kidneys). | 'Purpose of life' traumatized; refusal to acknowledge unresolved emotions and related issues.<br><br>When the hara region (front and back) is healed, 'we can *live with ourselves in harmony and peace*'—with those parts of ourselves which we do not like such as the alcoholic, the one who is a failure, the one who flirts too much or talks too much after a drink or two, the one who 'tolerates too much/is too giving', etc.<br><br>All these fragments of our selves reside at the *hara* region weakening our abilities to achieve and create. Past emotional hurts *thought over,* meditated upon and consequent *pain*—all accumulate here, damaging our purpose of life.<br><br>The **hara** is a key healing area, and also the place of the *false ego (ahankaar)—the illusory identification that 'I am the controller and doer'. (See the 'Five Principles of Reiki' and the 'Universal Energy Principles' for further elaboration.)* |

*'Reiki channels are not "doctors" . . . never discourage the healee from continuing his on-going therapies, especially in severe or difficult conditions . . . Just add Reiki healing to the other measures taken, and you may be privileged to closely participate in the amazing and the extraordinary.'*

| Body Part | Disease + Emotions |
|---|---|
| | **Kidney Disorders:** Relationship problems and issues not dealt with/painful to deal with openly.<br>Very major area for healing our lives as our peaceful and successful progress in life depends on relationships being harmonious at all levels, starting with the relationship within ourselves, with our fragmented parts which stay in the *hara* region, and our own higher self from which we are disconnected (before Reiki). |
| 26. **Base of Spine/Root Chakra:** Essential bodily survival issues. Seat of *kundalini* energy<br>*Destiny and seed karma.* | **Growth Disorders** and basic health disorders come from root chakra.<br>(Skeletal system, circulatory system, bodily form and development.)<br>**Deep-rooted disease, karmic reactions.**<br>**Suicidal Tendencies:** come from a small or weak root chakra<br>**Drug Addictions:** Result in closing down of back heart chakra and root chakra. Thus, drug addicts find 'nothing is happening' in their lives as **destiny** remains profoundly unfulfilled and inactive. |

NOTE: Where there is no apparent cause for disease in terms of attitudinal or emotional position, or where it is very mildly present—the disease or disorder must be understood as being *deeply karmic* in nature, requiring persistent healing.

In such conditions it is useful to give full-body healing by two or more Reiki channels simultaneously—each covering the 31 point positions as often as needed.

***Do not give judgemental diagnosis to healees on this basis.***

# 19

# *Disease, Body and Destiny*

All disorders manifesting in the physical body appear first as functional disorders of the mental-emotional and health bodies in the aura. Even in the case of accidents and so on, there is a preparation of the field, as it were, which is made suitable circumstantially for the event to take place. The internal attitude and position of the individual determines the events.

Observed practically as through the clairvoyant abilities of *Sensei* Renoo Nirula it is seen that in any given situation the element of desire is the strongest and yet the most subtle governing factor. According to his desire in a particular situation, the individual *chooses* a course of action, expecting a result according to his desire-generated thinking.

This course of action draws a particular result, activates a particular series of related and inevitable consequences which may be very different from expectation. These results are 'destiny'.

Based on these events, destiny inspires the next desire in the individual based on his inner evolution, his level of consciousness and as according to the individual's previous karmic balance of desires.

*This combination is responsible for developing the individual's current attitude to his life and its events, his current desires, aspirations and goals.*

As a factual example in our experience—a wealthy father with three sons rewards the middle son's abilities and his fair-minded nature, and therefore transfers most of his assets in the son's name with the express instruction that the son should divide and share the assets equally with the brothers after the father's death.

The father dies and the middle brother can do three things depending on his inner evolution and desire:

(a) He may decide to keep all the money and assets to himself since *legally* they are his (a course favoured by his wife).

(b) He may keep the assets in his name, invest them and divide the income equally among the brothers (to which no one would object, and his wife's second choice!). Or—

(c) He may divide the assets equally among the brothers as desired by his father.

Each of the activities would generate a different karmic result for the brother having the father's assets. With Reiki healing, the brother took the option (c): as desired by his father.

Clairvoyantly checked, should he have exercised either of the other options, he would have generated serious negative reactions.

Similarly, when it comes to 'healing', the individual healee may exercise the option of not wanting to be healed or only to be partially healed.

His karmic pattern may be very strong for the negative and the healee may lose patience before regaining health sufficiently.

Reiki channels need to be generally aware of this mechanism which is a major factor governing end-results of healings.

Channels must also absolutely avoid perpetuating attitudes like, 'I healed this person', or a judgemental-superior attitude over the healee because that also limits healing by placing a conditionality of the false ego in the flow of unconditional Reiki.

Having said all this, we see that the final factor governing healing results is Divine Grace and Divine Will which are not stifled by our false egos or mistakes. However, healing results may be withheld or delayed, in order for the Reiki channel or the healee to learn and rectify his attitude.

At the same time, Divine Grace is another name for Reiki for it is of the quality of unconditional love. It goes beyond reason and is not bound by laws of karma and does, in fact, heal and dissolve material karma.

However, if the healee does not want to receive this, or does not want to open himself to the Divine, or *does not invite the Divine—Reiki,* then, *no amount of healing will make much difference,* and the Reiki channel may feel disappointed. For this reason at the beginning stages of Reiki work, all channels are strictly told, 'healing may be given only on being asked for, and there must be some appropriate energy exchange which represents a tangible attitude of gratitude on the part of the healee. This progresses healing work.'

In practise, the gross material body (*annamaya kosh* as identified by ayurveda) and subtle material bodies (*pranamaya kosh*) of living beings can be harmonized, healed with Reiki such that material contaminations or defects no longer obstruct the radiance of the spirit from shining through.

In practical terms, it means making Reiki energy available at the key areas of the body which are 'storage' areas of certain emotions, thinking, attitudes.

As these areas heal and harmonize with one's true inner spiritual nature through Reiki empowerment, this nature which is always pure, progresses the individual to higher levels and states of consciousness automatically. One becomes a 'better person, a *good* person'. Not in the sentimental, sugary-sweet goody-goody sense, but in the sense of permitting the inherent noble, loving and fearless qualities of the spirit to shine forth and permeate one's daily activities from the smallest to the most important things.

* * *

Disease of certain body parts or systems reflect '*dis*-ease' in our feelings, emotions, thoughts; a discomfort of our inner selves which is very subtle and yet very, very real. These are communications from our inner selves that something is not right in our feelings, thoughts.

Ignored, or not dealt with adequately, this accumulation of inner dis-ease slowly reaches down to the physical body and manifests as a mental-emotional-bodily disease, affecting specific body parts or systems.

As detailed in the previous section, these body parts are storage places of very specific types of emotional distress.

Healing these parts heals the subtle emotional body as well, and when this happens, the physical body releases toxins, biochemical accumulations that were the immediate proximate causes of the disease. This is termed as a 'cleansing'—a discharge of toxic waste and a very good sign, although it may be somewhat uncomfortable or unpleasant—nasal discharges, loose motions, fevers and inflammatory conditions.

Typically, they pass in a short period of time, leaving the healee in a far better condition than he was earlier.

If at this time the healing treatments are increased, and some support therapies used such as ayurvedic, homeopathic and Bach Flower Remedies, etc., these serve to cut short the duration and intensity of the cleansing.

The intensity of the cleansing may also be reduced further by doing special healings (as via the Reiki Box and other advanced methods available to Reiki-2 channels) where the healing request is that, 'All cleansing reactions *have taken place* outside the aura of (healee's name) and gone back to the source of origin as love and light.' (This is covered in further detail in the section on *Affirmations and Intentions* and the *Reiki Box*.)

The following section lists diseases and the areas which require healing. For chronic diseases, full-body Reiki is essential at the Reiki-1 level. Reiki-2 has advanced methods available whereby the full-body Reiki time may be reduced to 15 or 20 minutes as compared to a normal full touch-body Reiki session of about 90 minutes. At the conclusion of the healing session, balancing of the chakras on the spine is desirable.

The balancing procedure itself is a powerful mini-healing, suitable for all acute problems, and some chronic ones like headaches (including migraines). The site or originating site of the problem is given Reiki for a few minutes, the six major chakras on the spine and the knees are given Reiki, and then the chakras balanced according to the procedure detailed in the relevant section. (For example, the originating site for migraines is emotional indigestion at the liver-gall-bladder, not the head.)

A **functional** disorder heals faster than a settled pathological disorder. For example a 'slipped' disc problem may take a long time to heal, but the accompanying pain, inflammation, etc., *can be relieved rapidly with Reiki.* 'Genetic' problems mean hardened *karma,* severe inherited tendency, and therefore may also require 'hard' measures such as surgery or other such treatment, or there may be some absolute limit of organic improvement, or there may be much DELAY. However, *there are no limits to the healing process—The person can be healed and be in harmony regardless of the end-result!* One may be healed and peacefully let go of the body which has worn out, or one may be healed internally, even while the physical healing or reversal of the physical condition may apparently be delayed.

# 20

# Repertory of Diseases: Reiki Points and Feedback

Diseases and their connection to bodily areas and Reiki points are listed for handy reference. Please remember that the best guide to healing is always your 'feedback': whether from hands or any of the other ways discussed earlier.

For example, Rati, a Reiki channel with diabetes had little success in reducing her blood sugar level with continued self-healing. She had been diligently Reiki'ing herself, especially at the spleen and pancreas, and the solar plexus areas.

On discussing her condition (and internally requesting Reiki to reveal the triggering and root causes for her diabetes—*very important!*), Rati volunteered that ever since her husband began travelling out of town on work five days of the week, she had been very afraid of being alone at night.

Her growing children used to sleep in the same room with her at night, but they had left home to study out of town. Her diabetes surfaced a few weeks after this. We advised her to Reiki the knee-calf chakras (for fear, anxiety; and the inability to adjust to changing conditions—not moving forward) and root chakra (deep karmic causes of disease) extensively. She also received the Bach Flower Remedies: Mimulus, for fear, and Walnut for healing past links that prevent moving forward.

A few days later her blood sugar level had dropped significantly. The key point exemplified here is that although the sites of the functional disorder or disease may receive sufficient Reiki, if the *root* of the problem is not sufficiently tackled and healed, relief and reversal of disease will not be 'whole and complete'.

*How can we find the root of the problem?* Internally request Reiki to guide you, ask relevant questions, and allow your 'feedback' mechanism to guide you; it will tell you which area requires the maximum healing. This may be through your hands, or an intuition, or by asking a few appropriate questions.

There is a specific method of asking questions in order to receive meaningful replies. If we ask questions that are in themselves suggestive of an answer, the reply would not be reliable, because most people tend to answer such questions according to the suggestion in-built into the question—it gives them an idea of what you are looking for, and they may give you a 'tailored' or manufactured reply which does not reflect the true situation.

Therefore, *avoid* asking questions like, 'Does your condition get worse with changes in the weather?' Sometimes all our conditions worsen during weather changes, but we would not think of answering so, unless it was very remarkably so. Thus their answering in the positive would be misleading.

Ask instead: 'Is there any pattern to your feeling better or worse . . . does anything make it better or worse?' This is open-ended and does not suggest a *specific* answer. In this case if the person volunteers, 'Every time the weather changes, or it rains, the problem gets aggravated,' or, if he says, 'This problem comes in March-April and September-October,' or, 'every time I come back home the problem gets worse,' you can understand from this that the person is unable to adjust to a changed condition or environment.

This general condition would guide you to Reiki the person's calves and knees more and use Walnut from the Bach Flower Remedies.

General conditions include specifics. Therefore, learn to generalize from specifics since the general all-inclusive condition tells us what the root cause of the problem is. At the same time, avoid too much questioning and too much generalizing.

For instance, while it is true that all our material disease originates as a problem of the heart, of love—in practice, we must Reiki other blocked areas as well, in order to effect rapid healings and disease reversals.

Be in harmony with the healing process and the chanelling of loving energies. Learn to listen to and trust your inner voice and guidance. This and your hands will tell you more than any number of questions can.

Always request Reiki to guide you.

‘Healing energy flows “on demand” from the healee’s inner needs. The Reiki channel must remember this... the Fourth Grandmaster often compares this to breast-feeding a baby.’

‘The mother does not decide she will dispense (for example) 1.25 ounces or 35 or 40 millilitres of milk to the baby like a machine. The baby takes as much as is needed.’

‘That is the position of so-called Reiki healers: they *make available* the healing energy in the best possible way for the results desired. And it is their commitment to results, their attitude of gratitude, that prevails.’

*—Renoo Nirula*

# 21

# *Healing in Emergency Conditions*

*In emergencies, administer appropriate first-aid measures and call for medical help.* Give Reiki healing at the main areas as listed. Besides these areas, there may be other points needing healing—follow your feedback.

If there is no feedback, or there is doubt, following the given positions will bring sufficient relief and results.

*In all emergencies* the • **solar plexus** chakras (front and back), • **back heart** chakra, and • **root** chakra are primarily involved. • **Knee** chakras are also involved. *All these points can be Reiki'd if you are not sure where to Reiki. You may also directly Reiki the pain/injury area (and the knees).*

Remember, Reiki will always go where needed most, and especially *in an emergency.* Even if you are not sure where to place your hands, just holding the other's hand or putting your hand on any part of their body will always make the healing energy available to the healee.

*In such a situation do not think that you didn't do enough or you made a 'mistake'. Whatever Reiki healing is possible in any situation, is a positive gain only—no loss.* With practise and 'hands-on' experience you will very soon be a competent and confident Reiki channel!

So remember: *Just do it—Just Reiki it!*

## Standard Emergency Chakra (SEC) Positions

1. Solar plexus
2. Back heart
3. Root
4. Knees

These are the *Standard Emergency Chakra* (*SEC*) positions for all acute problems/emergency conditions.

Positions 1, 2 and 3 are of greatest importance. These points (1 through 3) may be Reiki'd in any order, preferably starting with *solar plexus* and *back heart together—with one hand at each point*. The *italicized* chakra positions in the '*Disease: Reiki Points Repertory*' following, indicates important areas for ***acute*** conditions (e.g., high fever) or life threatening ones (e.g., heart attack).

In *all* manifest health conditions, the *solar plexus* chakra is always first involved, then the *heart* and *root* chakras.

Please Note: Nothing in this *Living Handbook of Reiki* is meant to be taken as a substitute for primary or additional sound health measures.

# 22

# *Disease: Reiki Points Repertory*

## Acute or Emergency Conditions

| Disease | Main Body Area |
| --- | --- |
| Abortion, threatened | SEC Positions, *Hara* |
| Angina | SEC Positions |
| Apoplexy (stroke) | SEC Positions + Third eye, temples, *Root* |
| Appendicitis | *Solar plexus, Hara, Root, Knees* |
| Asthma | *Solar plexus, Back heart,* Lung tips, (*Knee*) |
| Blood pressure, high or low | *Back hara, Solar plexus,* Kidneys (esp. high B.P.), Root (*esp. low B.P.*), Knees |
| Bronchitis, broncho-pneumonia | *Lung tips, Solar plexus, Liver, Root, Knees* |

| Disease | Main Body Area |
|---|---|
| Burns and scalds<br>Cuts and bruises | **Minor injury**: *Site* of the injury; **Major injury**: *Site* of injury (if possible), Solar plexus, Root, *Knees*<br><br>If injured part is sensitive, the hands may be held a few inches away. (See adjacent illustration.) |

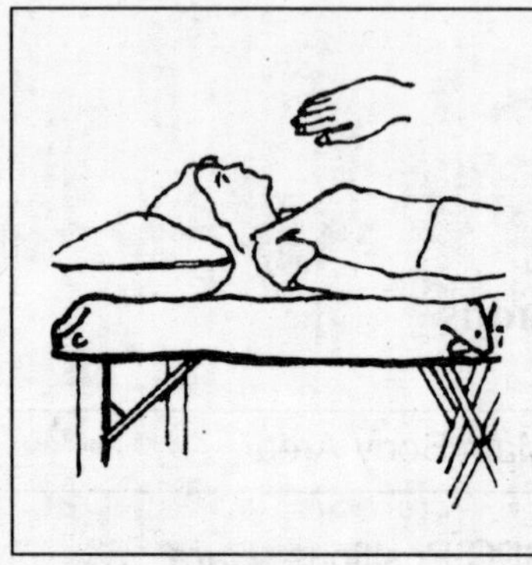

| Disease | Main Body Area |
|---|---|
| Diarrhoea<br>Dysentery | *Solar plexus, Liver, Hara, Root*, (Knees) |
| Delirium/Fainting (shock/injury) | *SEC positions** |
| Gastro-enteritis | *Solar plexus, Liver, Hara, Root*, (Knees) |

Heart attack symptoms : Acute to moderate pain in chest and left arm, sweating and pallor; breathlessness, general anxiety, palpitations.

---

**(SEC) Standard Emergency Chakra Positions:*
1. Solar Plexus; 2. Back Heart; 3. Root; 4. Knees.

| Disease | Main Body Area |
|---|---|

**Heart attack**

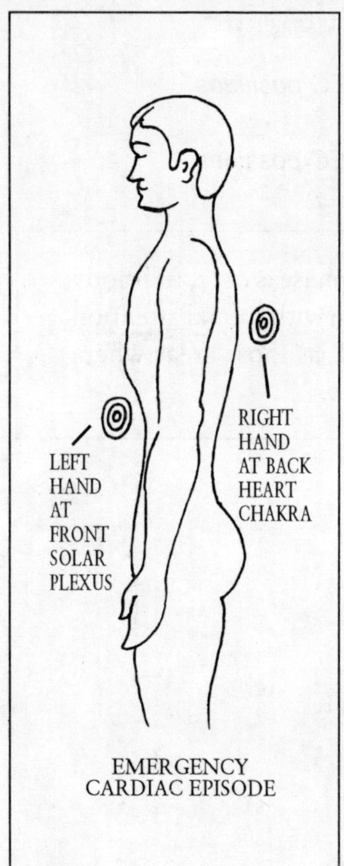


***SEC Positions:***

**First**: Reiki with one hand on *the back heart* chakra (never the front), of healee, the other hand on *front solar plexus* chakra.

**Next**: Desire and mentally request Reiki to open and keep healee's back heart chakra open.

**When Relieved** (or as appropriate): Reiki the knees **while continuing Back Heart chakra Reiki.**

(Additionally you may invoke the 'Divine Reiki Light Distance Healing' procedure. p. 183)

**Immediately seek medical attention/take healee to a hospital/ nursing home as may be appropriate.**

| Disease | Main Body Area |
|---|---|
| Hysteria | *Solar plexus,* Back heart, Third eye, (Calves and knees) |
| Miscarriage *(see 'Abortion')* | |
| Poisoning | *SEC positions** |
| Shock and Stress | *SEC positions** |

After the acute or emergency phase is over, full-body healing treatment may be given with special attention to the key areas listed, as well as those areas where you receive feedback guidance.

**(SEC) Standard Emergency Chakra Positions:*
**1. Solar Plexus; 2. Back Heart; 3. Root; 4. Knees.**

## Chronic or Recurrent Conditions

Chronic or recurrent conditions require *full-body* Reiki for at least 21 treatments (see p. 111, *'Doing Reiki Healing'—Healing Chronic Conditions: 21 Healings Cycle)*. The additional points listed here are the areas relating most to the condition in our experience.

**Please remember that other points as per individual conditions would also require healing.** *Allow your feedback to guide you.* (See: *'Doing Reiki Healing'* p. 111.) *Emphasized* points are recommended especially for *all* phases of the disease. For *all* disease conditions and states, *solar plexus*, *root*, *heart* and *knees* (*SEC* positions) are *always involved*. These points are understood as needing Reiki even when not indicated in the listings.

| Disease | Main Body Area |
|---|---|
| Abscess | *Liver,* Root, (and site) |
| AIDS | *Back thymus, Heart, Root,* Hara, Liver |
| Asthma | *Solar plexus, Back heart,* Lung tips, (*knees*) |
| Acidity | Solar plexus, Spleen, Liver, Knees, Kidneys |
| Acne | Liver, Hara, Root |
| Adenoids, Nasal polyps | Third eye, Root, (site) |
| Albumin in urine | Kidneys, Liver, Solar plexus, Root |
| Addictions | *Solar plexus, Calves*, Knees, Thighs |
| Anaemia | Root, Spleen, Solar plexus |
| Arthritis | *Back thymus*, Knees, Liver, Spleen + Pancreas, Hara, Kidneys |

| Disease | Main Body Area |
|---|---|
| Backaches | *Site* of pain, and *nearest related chakra (Back thymus / Back heart/ solar plexus–Kidneys/*hara), *Knees* |
| Bedsores | (Site of problem), Liver, Root, Knees |
| Bladder, irritable | Hara, Root, Knees |
| Boils | Liver, Solar plexus, Root |
| Bone diseases | Root, Liver, Solar plexus, Pancreas |
| Cervical spondylosis | Throat, Shoulders, Hara |
| Cough | Throat, Solar plexus, Liver, Root, (knees) |
| Cramps—calves/feet | Calves, Feet, Knees |
| Deafness—chronic | Ears, all head positions, Root, Ankles |
| Depression | *Hara, Liver,* Solar plexus, *Back heart* |
| Diabetes | *Solar plexus, Pancreas and spleen,* Liver, *Root,* (knees) |
| Ear, diseases of | *Ears*, All head positions, *Root*, Liver |
| Eczema | *Liver*, *Hara*, Solar plexus, Spleen, Root, Knees |
| Epilepsy | Third eye, (all head positions), Root |

**(SEC) Standard Emergency Chakra Positions:*
1. Solar Plexus; 2. Back Heart; 3. Root; 4. Knees.

| Disease | Main Body Area |
|---|---|
| Eye, diseases of | *Eyes*, Occipital lobes (back of head), Solar plexus, Liver, Root |
| Fever | Solar plexus, Liver, Root, (hara, *knees*) |
| Impotence/infertility | *Kidneys, Hara, Root,* Spermatic cords/ovaries, (knees) |
| Inflammations | *Solar plexus, Liver* (hara), *Root* |
| Insomnia | *Ears, Solar plexus,* Knees, Kidneys |
| Kidney diseases | Kidneys, Root chakra, Hara |
| Malnutrition | *Root,* Solar plexus, (heart) |
| Miscarriage | See 'Abortion' |
| Morning sickness | Liver, Solar plexus, Root, *Calves* |
| Nerve and brain disorders (including Alzheimer's, Parkinson's, etc.) | *Third eye, Hara, Root,* and other points as per guidance |
| Osteoporosis | *Root, Hara, Liver,* Solar plexus, Pancreas |
| Paralysis | *Back heart, Hara,* Root, Third eye (+head positions if stroke) |
| Pimples | *Hara, Liver,* Root, Kidneys (calves—at puberty) |
| Prostrate, disease of | Hara, Spermatic cords, Root |
| Pregnancy—*disturbances during* | *Hara, Calves,* Knees, *Solar plexus, Liver,* Heart |

| Disease | Main Body Area |
|---|---|
| Relationship issues | *Kidneys*, Hara, Knees, Solar plexus |
| Rheumatism | See 'Arthritis' |
| Senile changes | Third eye, Root, Solar plexus |
| Sciatica *(see also under 'Backache')* | Hara, Kidneys, Knees |
| Shock | SEC positions* |
| Skin, diseases of | *Liver, Hara*, Spleen + Pancreas, *Kidneys* |
| Sleeping sickness | *Third eye, Root,* Liver, Solar plexus |
| Sleeplessness | See 'Insomnia' |
| Tonsilitis | *Throat, Hara, Liver* |
| Toothache | *Site of pain*, Root chakra, *Knees (esp. visiting the dentist)* |
| Travel sickness | *Liver, Knees, Solar plexus,* (calves, ankles) |
| Urticaria | See under 'Skin' |
| Vertigo | *Ankles*, Ears, Eyes |

**(SEC) Standard Emergency Chakra Positions:*
1. Solar Plexus; 2. Back Heart; 3. Root; 4. Knees.

# 23

# 'Healing Procedures'

## 'Self-healing Procedures'

To begin:

1. Wash hands as may be appropriate. *During all healings, ensure that your legs/feet are not crossed.*

2. State and be in the Attitude of Gratitude. ***'I thank myself for being here. I thank Reiki for being here. I thank*** (your name) ***for being here. Reiki please make*** (your name) healed ***whole and complete. So it is. Thank you. Thy/Divine Will be done.'***

3. You may do Reiki while lying down or sitting. If any position requires it, change to an appropriate position. For example, while doing the back body positions, it is better to lean back. This eliminates a forward bending posture which can congest the upper chest and make you feel uncomfortable and may lead you to avoid doing the back positions or lessen the time.

   Please remember—*the back positions are most important*, because the back chakras are the input points for energy, whereas the front chakras are the output. If the back (input) chakras are not clear and healed, the energy outflow will not take place properly. *Begin with the front body positions.* Start the healing procedure by laying of *cupped hands* according to the sequence. Desire that you, the person, should be healed.

4. Wait for the feedback, *or three minutes at least*, at each position.

   If at any time your hands are drawn away or you are guided to move them to another place away from, but near the starting position, *allow this to happen.*

   But remember that the technically correct position should also be given Reiki healing for a short while.

5. When you feel complete with the current position, move gently on to the next position.

6. After completing the sequence, if you feel you need to go back to some previously done position, do so.

7. After the front body positions, complete the *back body* positions.

8. After completing the back, internally state and be in the *Closing Attitude of Gratitude.* I '(your name) ***is healed, whole and complete . . . thank you. So it is. Thy/ Divine Will be done. I thank Reiki, I thank myself, I thank*** (your name).'

9. This completes the *Full-body Reiki Self-healing treatment.*

This concludes the summary for Full-body Self-healing Reiki treatment.

## Healing Others: Front Body

To begin:

1. Wash hands. *During all healing, ensure healee's and your legs/feet are not crossed.*
2. Internally state and be in the Attitude of Gratitude. ***'I thank myself for being here. I thank Reiki for being here. I thank** (healee's name) **for being here. Reiki please make** (healee's name) **healed whole and complete. So it is. Thank you. Thy/ Divine Will be done.'***
3. The person being treated should best (most conveniently) be lying down. *Begin with the front body positions.* Start the healing procedure by laying of cupped hands according to the sequence. *Desire the person be healed.*
4. Wait for the feedback, *or about three minutes*, at each position. If at any time your hands are drawn away or you are guided to move them to another position away from, but near the starting position, *allow this to happen.*
5. When you feel complete with the current position, move gently on to the next position, one hand at a time, always maintaining contact with the healee's body.
6. After completing the sequence, if you feel you need to go back to some previously done position, please do so.
7. On completing the front body Reiki, take a position where the *healee's head is to your right.* This is

important. If necessary *ask the healee to adjust his position* so that his head is to your right when he is lying on his back. (In future, you can remember to position the healee such that this naturally happens.)

8. For the next procedure, practise drawing anti-clockwise spirals in the air with the first two fingers of your right hand. (You may practise now if you like.) In all energy work, use only anti-clockwise spirals. Be sure that these are anti-clockwise spirals—you will be surprised at how often we (and others) may get it wrong! If you make a mistake in this anti-clockwise procedure, mentally recall and cancel it. There will be no harm. If possible re-do it.

9. *Draw rapid anti-clockwise* spirals a few inches from the healees' body with the *first two fingers* of your right hand:

   1. Down from nearest shoulder to fingers.
   2. Down from nearest shoulder to toes.
   3. Down from farther shoulder to toes.
   4. Down from farther shoulder to fingers.

   ***Finish*** by drawing **three-and-a-half** anticlockwise ellipses (ovals) with your hand, palm facing downwards, about nine inches (20 cm) above the healee's body, **starting** from the toes and moving up around and down the head, **ending** at the level of the heart near the shoulder (not above heart).

This concludes the summary for giving front body Reiki treatment.

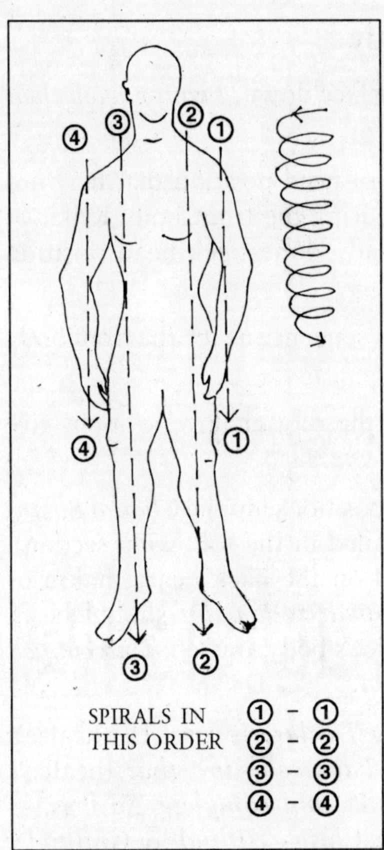


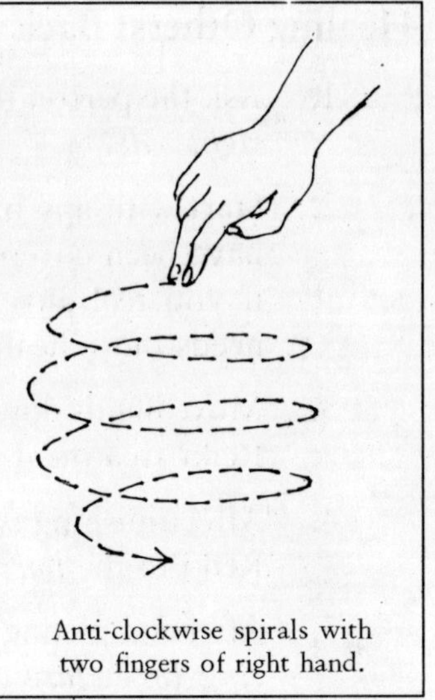

Anti-clockwise spirals with two fingers of right hand.

**Note:**
Spirals/ellipses are always drawn anti-clockwise.

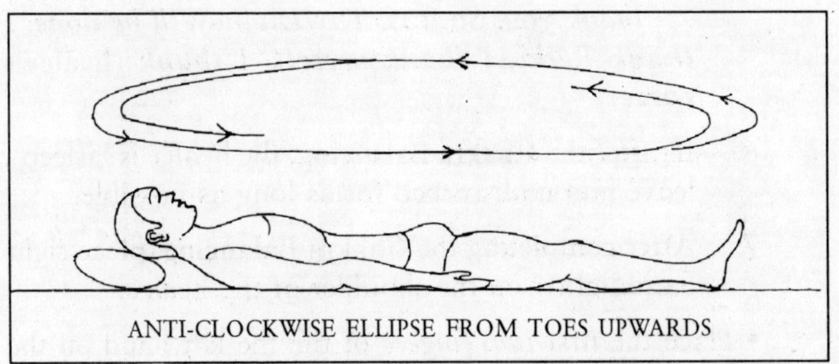

ANTI-CLOCKWISE ELLIPSE FROM TOES UPWARDS

## Healing Others: Back Body

1. Ask the person to lie face down, *turning from their right side.*

2. Start with any back of head position that may not have been covered during the front body Reiki, or if you feel any already done back-head position needs more healing.

3. Move hands down in sequence as for the front body Reiki treatment.

4. After finishing with the root chakra position, give Reiki to the *back of knees.*

5. After completing all positions, do the *Chakra Balancing Procedure* (detailed in the following section), finishing with hands on the back heart chakra of the healee. The *cupped right palm* should be in contact with the healee's body, the *left hand cupped over the healer's right.*

   Make the *Balancing Declaration* • '*All* (healee's name) *chakras are balanced, and that* (healee's name) *is healed, whole and complete. So it is.*'—and *complete with* the *Closing Attitude of Gratitude.* • '(Healee's name) ***is healed, whole and complete . . . thank you. So it is. Thy/DivineWill be done. I thank Reiki, I thank myself, I thank*** (healee's name).'

6. If, after the Chakra Balancing, the healee is 'asleep', leave him undisturbed for as long as possible.

7. **After completing the Chakra Balancing,** place right hand lightly on the shoulder of the healee.

• Place the first *two fingers* of the the left hand on the seventh cervical vertebra on the spine—the back throat chakra. • Maintaining *firm* contact, rapidly bring the fingers down to the *root* chakra drawing a line from top to bottom. • Do this three times. (*For diabetics the lines are drawn down twice, and then from the root chakra up towards the neck once.*) This procedure removes residual negative energy from the spinal chakras via the root chakra. • *Conclude* with a smart pat at the root chakra with the palm of your hand. This seals the root chakra so that the negative energy does not flow back. *Do not neglect this.*

Finish with a gentle loving touch from the top of the head to the feet. Tell the healee that he may get up whenever he likes. Wash your hands. This completes the giving of *Full-body Reiki* healing treatment to others.

This concludes the complete summary of giving Full-body Reiki healing treatment to others.

> *Note:* Our attention has been drawn to other balancing systems and methods: please be careful as most of those methods incorrectly pair the chakras, or succeed in wrongly raising the kundalini, especially where figure-of-eight type lines are drawn on the back. Above all: *Please remember—Chakras can* ***never*** *be balanced from the front by touch!*

## Chakra Balancing/Quick Healing

**Chakra Balancing** is to be done at every full-body Reiki session for the healee. It can also create an 'instant' state of well-being in many acute conditions without the need for full-body Reiki. **Remember**: Serious conditions require *Full-body Reiki.*

• **For Rapid Relief/Quick Healing:** Chakra Balancing is a very quick-healing method for many acute problems which may also require Reiki directly on the affected areas. After giving Reiki to the affected area, balance the chakras on the spine as detailed. • *If only Chakra Balancing is to be done, always invoke the Opening and Closing Attitude of Gratitude.*

## The Procedure

The following pairs of chakras are to be balanced on the spine:

1. Back Third Eye and Root Chakras
2. Throat and Hara Chakras
3. Heart and Solar Plexus Chakras

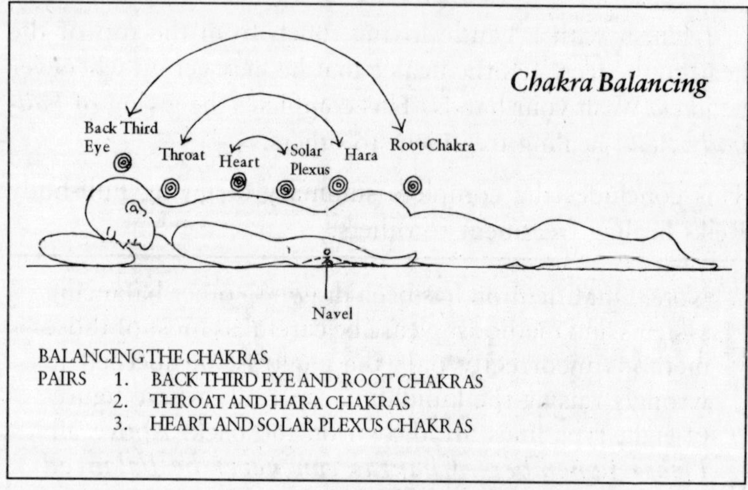


While balancing the chakras, *keep in mind the intention that you are balancing the particular pair of chakras.*

**Always take care to balance these pairs in this sequence only. In case of errors, mentally cancel the procedure and re-do it.**

*'Quick Method' of Chakra Balancing:*

1. Place your lightly cupped right palm on healee's back third eye chakra gently, while placing your lightly cupped left palm gently on healee's root chakra.

2. Slowly allow your hands to rise up—at some point you may feel a change in sensation in your hands—

pause there. If you do not feel any sensation, pause anywhere from a couple of inches (5 cm) above the healee's body to up to about ten inches (25 cm) above healee's body, keeping both palms level with each other.

3. Mentally declare: '(Healee's name's) *third eye and root chakras are balanced, so it is.'*
4. Now, without touching healee's body move your right cupped palm above and over the healee's back hara Pause.
5. Mentally declare: '(Healee's name's) *throat Chakra and harà àre balanced, so it is.'*
6. Without touching healee's body move your right palm above and over healee's heart chakra, and bring your left hand a few centimetres (an inch or two) away from your right hand—thus placing it above and over healee's solar plexus chakra.
7. Mentally declare: '(Healee's name's) *heart and solar plexus chakras are balanced, so it is, thank you.'*
8. Place your right cupped palm lightly on healee's heart chakra area on his back, then place your left palm on top of your right.
9. Mentally declare: '(Healee's name) *chakras are balanced, he is healed whole and complete, so it is, thank you, Thy Will be done . . . etc. (Closing AOG).'*
10. Then with your right hand on healee's shoulder, with the first two fingers of the left hand firmly draw three vertical lines down the centre of the spine all the way to the root (to discharge negative energies) and then with your left palm smartly pat the root chakra closed.

11. If the healee has diabetes, then draw two lines down, and the third up—patting the root chakra closed. (This helps prevent sudden drop in blood sugar levels.)
12. With both hands gently touch the healee from head to foot in a gentle loving motion, distributing the energies evenly.
13. Internally thank healee, Reiki, yourself, etc.
14. This is the quick method of balancing chakras. Tell the healee he may get up whenever he wishes. Wash your hands.

*Temporary Chakra Balancing/'Instant Healing'*

*Details are in the Advanced Knowledge Sealed Section at end—do not open until having practised these methods and done self-healing for at least one week.*

24

# Emotional-Energy Principles, Effects and Causes, 'Karma'

1. **Energy follows desire and thought**

   We experienced that in our bodies wherever we direct our thoughts or desires, energy follows it. In our lives as well, energy follows desires and thoughts which motivate us to do certain things, to achieve certain goals.

2. **Like attracts like**

   We multiply and attract what we meditate on—positive ☺ *or* ☹ negative. It is common experience that a type of emotion or thought generates its similar thought and feeling. Laughter or happiness is infectious, as is depression or a sad state of emotional being.

   *Similarly, 'karma' is fashioned according to our own desire to experience a certain emotional state.* In order to fulfill that, events start manifesting. When this happens we may not like the *how* of what is happening—the events attached to it which make us experience the emotional state. For example, one may desire what it feels like to experience the state of being waited upon for one's every need (to be a 'lord' or 'master').

The resultant events being fashioned may vary from experiencing this as a patient in a luxury nursing home with every possible medical attention, to having millionaire parents affording this attention from numerous servants, but no attention from the busy parents. What one gets depends on how much accumulated *karma* one has available to 'pay' for this. Therefore, we may not like the events that fashioned this destiny although we wanted *one specific* aspect of it and *desired* it.

3. **'Life events are fashioned by our desires** This happens in conjunction with our *karmic* bank-balance. Empowered by *Reiki,* one can radically change this, spiritually evolving, healing oneself: 'becoming whole and complete and thus changing the circumstances, the results of *past karma* of their lives, and the past *karmas* themselves. Just as the body is a result of our inner condition, life is a mirror of our inner condition in action. *Healing ourselves internally heals our life externally.* With *Reiki* we can create a positive present and future—This is what it means to be a 'Master of one's destiny'.

4. ***Good* and *Bad*, *Right* and *Wrong* depends on our perception of consequences'**

   As our current perception or judgement changes, so does our perception of 'good-bad', 'right-wrong'. What we classify as 'bad/wrong' today, may well be 'good/right' tomorrow and vice versa. When we ask for something to be set 'right', or 'healed', how do we avoid negative *karma?* In other words, ***what standard should we follow?*** . . .

   For example, our Reiki channels had been requesting Reiki to *heal* the political scenario for the greater benefit of the country's populace, and the environment of New Delhi since July 1995, and in early 1996 the effects were strongly visible as a major shake-up, a cleansing in the political area, with the judiciary becoming very active in all these areas. Reiki channels worldwide report similar results for healing terrorism and the political situation.

If we take a *judgemental* position, apportioning 'blame' and actively interfering in someone's life-pattern, we may have to digest the consequences. *Having taken the position of a judge,* ***we shall also attract judgement upon ourselves*** *according to our real inner motivation, by the principle of* ***'like attracts like'***.

Hence, *drop* 'judgemental-ism', dealing with the situation completely, dissolving all emotional negativism attached to it. Therefore, no more: 'My tension/ headache/heart problem/(. . . current ailment. . .) is thanks to you—because of what you did to me,' and so on. *Drop judging that unlikeable part of you* which you hold responsible for your bad behaviour and activities, because that is 'the other' you, the 'other' part of you which is *fragmented* away. Heal and integrate yourself, not condemning and not being guilty. *Guilt energies are very heavy*—forgive yourself for everything and love all parts of yourself unconditionally, *the same way Reiki comes to you unconditionally.*

5. **Blaming 'others', or depending on others emotionally means no change in our position**

Blaming 'others' does not shift us from our position, whether these others are outsiders or our own fragmented parts.

*As Reiki Channels we may no longer hold responsible our horoscope, the planets, God or anyone else for* ***our emotional indigestion and life-situation.***

Transferring responsibility elsewhere means the situation cannot change since *I am unwilling* to change it, as I hold 'someone or something else' responsible who will come and change it. *This doesn't happen!* On the other hand, *depending on Reiki gives us all the practical results we are looking for, provided, 'Just for today, I shall do my work honestly.'*

A Reiki Channel or a 'Master of one's own destiny' means taking *full responsibility for oneself* in all things in life.

# 25

# *Intention Reiki and Reiki Box*

*I*ntentions, desires and thoughts attract energies. *'Energy follows thought.'*

With Reiki empowerment, this attraction is multiplied manifold. This means that in effect what a Reiki channel intends or thinks *IT IS SO! To the extent of the Reiki channel's capacity to channel energy, to that extent the thought or intention appears in the external world. This is a major and key fundamental.*

- Avoid making negative statements such as: 'This person will never do well in his studies . . . he can't study . . . he is stupid! . . . I am not getting better—Reiki is not working . . . etc. . . .'—*because these will all manifest as self-fulfilling prophecies!*
- *If a negative thought process appears in your consciousness towards a person or event, strongly intend that it is* **neutralized** *by stating internally or verbalizing: 'Recall and cancel (the thought).'*
- *Focus on positivities stating them in the present-perfect tense.* Thus, we would *declare* that a person is healed *now, not* that he will be healed tomorrow. Or, we may positively and firmly state: '**(healee's name) is healed, whole and complete . . . / . . . lives in complete abundance.** . . . etc.' In difficult conditions you may request healing for a specific problem such as 'heart disease'—but

remember that the **general healing statement** ***('healee is healed whole and complete')*** **must always be included.**

- You may also conveniently give Reiki across time and space through the **Reiki Box.**
- **Intentions/situations/persons** may also be Reiki'd according to the procedure for sending healing across time and space *(p. 179)*.

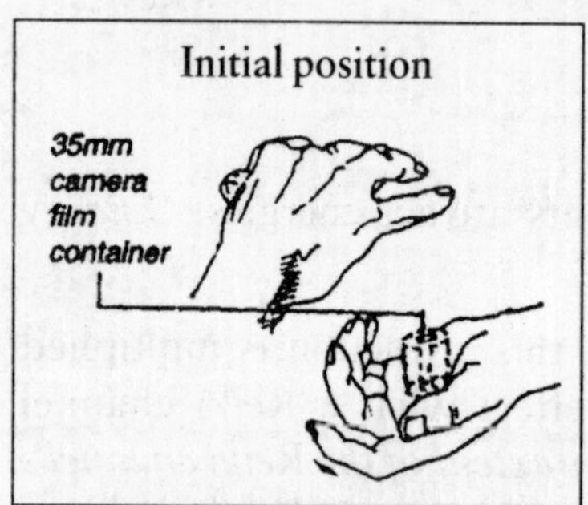


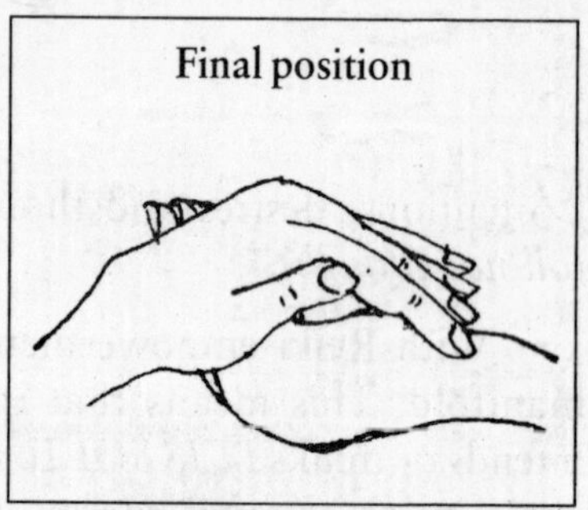


**Reiki Box:** Take a small non-metallic box with a tight fitting lid. A 35 mm roll-film plastic container is ideal. Any *intentions* you want to Reiki, including healees, can each be written on a separate slip of paper and placed in the container or box. Reiki the box for at least 10 minutes a day, requesting in the **Opening Attitude of Gratitude** that *'Reiki please make* (your name)'s *Reiki Box and the intentions in it healed, whole and complete, so it is, thank you . . . etc. . . '*. In the **Closing Attitude of Gratitude** state: '(Your name)'s *Reiki Box and the intentions in it are healed, whole and complete, so it is, thank you, Thy Will be done . . .' (thank Reiki, the Reiki Box, the intentions, etc.)*

When the intentions **manifest,** or are time-barred, *burn the intention slip*. This is very important, as it completes and concludes the energy cycle relating to that intention. (Dispose off the ashes in a plant, or in the kitchen sink with water.)

# 26

# Intentions and Affirmations

Affirmations may be made for healing. These affirmations are *intentions* that you may want to materialize, and are all stated in the *present perfect tense, as having being achieved now.* This is so even if the event is a future one or a past one. Some of the most powerful healing affirmations are:

- '(Healee's name . . .) lives in complete abundance of health, wealth, happiness and joy—so it is (thank you, Thy Will be done).'
- '. . . has forgiven his/her past and all those connected with it—so it is. . . .'
- '. . . loves himself/herself as he/she is and forgives himself/herself—so it is. . .'
- '. . . has accepted divine Reiki healing and the process of being healed....'

A mental or spoken Affirmation or Intention is in itself a very powerful form of healing as it is Reiki empowered. Further empowerment may be made through the Reiki Box and/or through the Divine Reiki Light method.

*Give the intentions and affirmations sufficient time to manifest.* Avoid giving deadline dates as far as possible. In the case of naturally time-barred situations such as an interview, meeting or examination, the date can be stated in the following manner: '**(healee's name's) meeting** ***scheduled*** for October 15th is healed whole and complete with results in the best interests of (healee's name) . . . So it is, thank you, etc.' Or, '. . . (healee's name) has studied for and performed perfectly in the exams and received the best results . . . etc.'

*Healing affirmations can be made for healing a person, a situation, a relationship, or for* **creating** *a situation or relationship. For example:*

- '(Healee's name) and his (wife's/husband's/friend's name) relationship is healed whole and complete, so it is, thank you, Thy Will be done.'
- '. . . (name's) board meeting/court case on (date) is healed whole and complete . . . etc.'
- '. . . argument/dispute between *(name)* and (name) and their relationship is healed, whole and complete. . . . So it is, thank you, (etc.).'
- '. . . has got married to the best and most compatible husband/wife. So it is. . . .' *(This may be stated even when there is no one yet on the scene—the right person will soon manifest.)*
- '. . . all (names) activities during the week/month of *(specify)* are healed whole and complete. . . .' (You can also place your hands at the appropriate place on your calender while doing this—'*Calender Reiki*'. You may Reiki a specific activity marked or scheduled on your calendar for success and being whole and complete.)

All affirmations are stated in the **present perfect** tense, as having been already achieved ***now.*** This is so even if the event is a **future** one or a **past** one. Affirmations made in **general/ global terms** have a wider scope of action and often manifest faster.

If the **specific** intention did not manifest then affirm the intention **globally in general terms**—in other words, as far as possible **do not limit it** by saying, for example, '(healee's name) has got the best possible job *with Alfred Beta Corporation*'— because a better job may be waiting with *Xavier Yum-yum Zeta! Such is very often the case.*

A *global ongoing intention* such as for 'Abundance. . . ' is considered manifest the day you get the feeling, the thought— ' My life is really great. . . . Thank you Reiki. . .' At that time: *burn the affirmation, re-write it, and put it in the Reiki Box. A new level of benefits will be achieved.*

If the intention does not manifest, re-consider your intention request. Do you really want it? If yes, then consider what else you may need to heal or do in your life in order that the intention should manifest. For example, if a person has cirrhosis of the liver and is drinking alcohol regularly and not stopping it, then Reiki will take a long time to get some result. By that time the person may have transited to his next body. *Reiki'ng something and not working for the results yourself may not get you the results desired*—***review the Fourth Principle of Reiki!***

Govind, a recently connected teenage Reiki channel doing very good healing for himself and his friends in school came for his Reiki-2 from South India. He was disappointed because his very important intention in the Reiki Box had not manifested, he said. He had wanted to be on the school basketball team and despite being a good player he was not chosen. Nalin asked him to state exactly what his intention in the Reiki Box said. Govind's intention was, 'I wish I was on the school basketball team.' Nalin smiled: 'Of course your intention was fulfilled—you are still wishing you were on the team, isn't it? If you were already on the team, there would be no more "wishing" . . . so always state—*this has already happened!* Otherwise you will keep on wishing. . . . We have to get out of this habit of tentatively asking, wishing, begging—putting responsibility on someone else—or God finally! Boldly state—*It has been done—Thank you Reiki!*'

*'Should we really be asking Reiki to fulfill our mundane, material desires. Isn't there something wrong in invoking divine energy for material things or "wrong" things?'*

NO! That is superficial understanding only. Ask for everything you ever wanted in life and *surrender* to *Reiki* for the results. Why? Simply because there are many unfulfilled desires within us that need healing, that create ill-health. Don't suppress them, rather, acknowledge them. Don't blame or condemn yourself for having these desires.

*No guilt please!* When you ask *Reiki* to fulfill these desires, one of two things will happen. The first is that *Reiki* will give you what you ask for and having received this you shall naturally be in an attitude of gratitude and develop further with *Reiki* in a particular direction.

The second is that *if it is not in your interest according to divine intelligence, or it is something that is so-called 'wrong'—then Reiki* will *not* give you your desire, but instead heal that part of you, that area from which that desire arises *so that you are free of it and become perfectly peaceful.* And then also you will be in an attitude of gratitude for having been freed from that desire, that itch, which would have normally increased the more you gave in to it—entangling you in further karmic reactions—if you did not have the *Reiki* empowerment. Either way, you gain enormously.

And finally, unless you Reiki *everything* in your life you will not be Karma-free quickly. Reiki'ng all your activities means being free of materially binding Karma.

So, freely, happily, gratefully ask for your heart's desire and leave the results to *Reiki* in an attitude of surrender.

# 27

# Sending Healing Across Space and Time

## The Divine Reiki Light Method 1

This procedure has been confidential so far, requiring special empowerment. We now empower and authorize all genuine Reiki channels worldwide to be able to invoke this procedure successfully in three ways: (i) if they receive this procedure through this authorized book, or (ii) through Reiki Masters created by us and further in this lineage, and (iii) where any genuine Reiki Master has accepted this procedure from this *Living Handbook of Reiki* and further conveyed it to their students *as it is, with no changes.* With this procedure Reiki-1 channels can send healing across space and time for the same effect as Reiki-2 channels. Reiki-2s can use this with the addition of the mystic symbols for more powerful effects. *This is an authentic procedure applicable to healing a person, a situation, a relationship—or for creating a situation or relationship that as yet does not exist.* (See also 'Reiki Box' and 'Intentions and Affirmations'.)

## The Procedure

1. Mentally request Reiki to send you the Divine Reiki Light (DRL). *(Do not specify any colour.)*

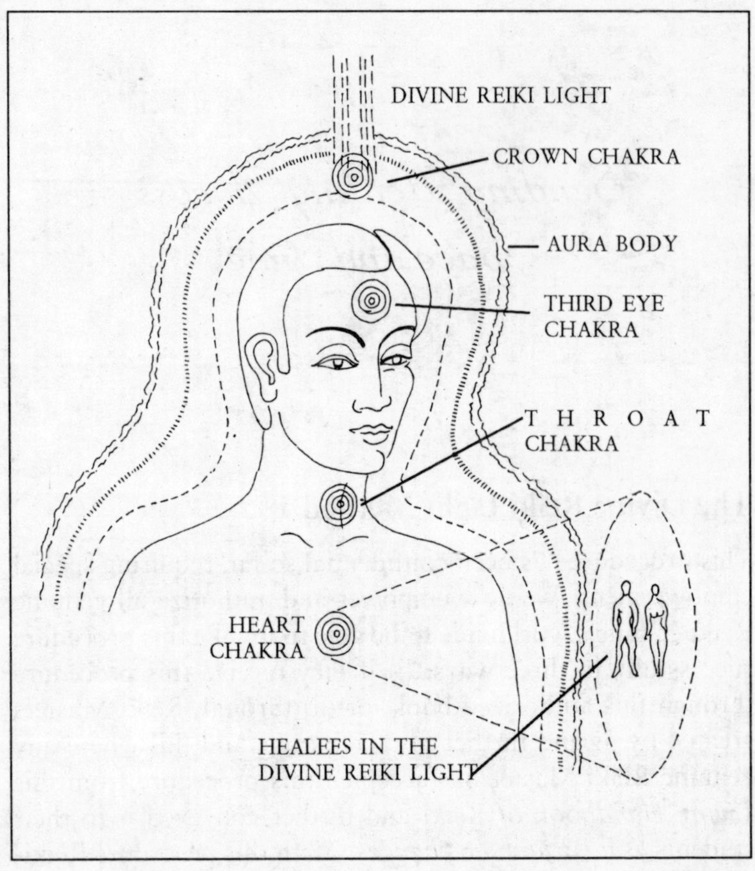


2. Intend the DRL is entering your crown chakra from above and comes down through the third eye and throat chakras to your heart chakra.

3. **Project** the DRL out from your front heart chakra in a cone-like fashion, like a flashlight beam, and *completely outside your aura in front* to form a circle of light about half a metre (about two feet) in diameter to cover the person, the intention, the situation. The healee intended is naturally sufficiently small in size so as to be covered by the DRL.

4. This is the basic procedure and can be enhanced further by sending additional healing through the hands as follows:

   4.1 Invoke the Attitude of Gratitude (AOG), requesting Reiki to heal the person, the intention, the situation.

   4.2 Intend that Reiki should *also* flow from your hands to heal the objective covered by the Divine Light (at closing state the Closing AOG, and also thanks the DRL).

5. *Get feedback*. For instance, you can intend/specify as feedback that the person receiving Reiki is *smiling, turning away or leaving* when the healing is done. When you *feel complete* with the healing, declare the person, intention, situation as healed, *closing with the attitude of gratitude.*

6. Thank the DRL with the request: *'Be with Reiki please.'* (*Do NOT send the Divine Reiki Light back to the source as love and light*!)

7. You can send healing this way to many people in a group.

8. Using this and the **Reiki Box** you can send healing across time—past, present or future—and space to a person, a situation, or for creating a new situation.

9. The healing time through the DRL varies from a few minutes to much longer.

10. EXPERIENCE is the best way to get a working understanding of how to use this procedure and how much healing to send.

11. Distance healing involves some 'transmission losses' and although relatively not as powerful as direct

touch healing or Reiki Box healing, it is still a very significant and powerful method, especially in emergencies or when direct touch healing cannot be given. A Reiki-2 invoking the DRL (with the mystic symbols) can have the same effect as a Reiki-1 giving touch healing—it is of such capacity.

Note:

- Sometimes after invoking the DRL for a healing, you may 'forget' that you have done this or become distracted for a while, and then you will suddenly remember that some healee was in the DRL and that you had completely forgotten about it. This may be a few minutes later or a few hours later—it doesn't matter. There will be no ill effect. This event takes place because the healee *needs* that much healing.

**Reiki Flowing through Hand Chakras into the Cone of Divine Reiki Light**

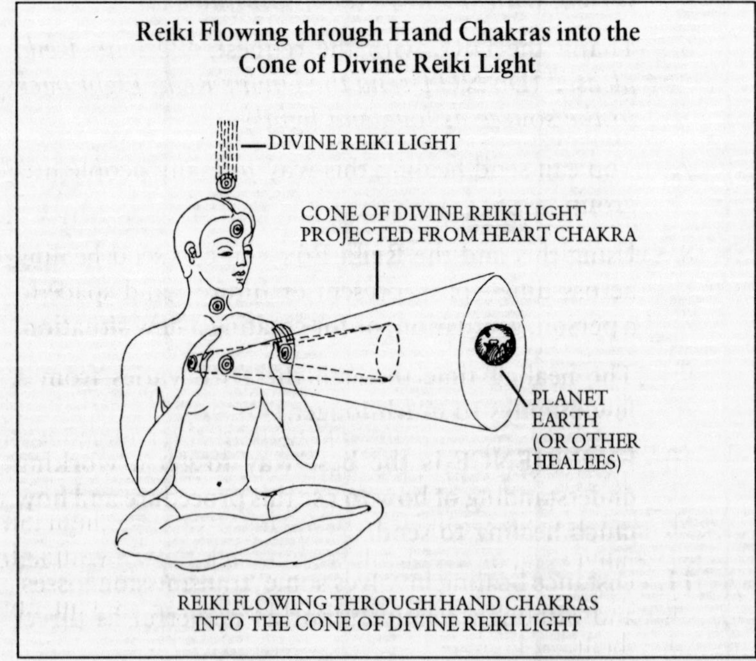


REIKI FLOWING THROUGH HAND CHAKRAS INTO THE CONE OF DIVINE REIKI LIGHT

- Whenever you remember, state the Closing Attitude of Gratitude and request the DRL to be with Reiki—even if this be the next day.
- The DRL can remain on continuously for six hours at a time, after which it disconnects and merges back with the Reiki within you. If you need to, you can immediately re-invoke the DRL after it terminates.

## The Divine Reiki Light Method 2

'Heal the World' Meditation

*(This may be done in a group sitting in a circle, while one person reads out this healing meditation's procedure in a soothing relaxed manner, . . . giving appropriate pauses where indicated by dots and anywhere else appropriate. This basic format can be elaborated further for specifics, but as a general healing this is sufficient.)*

1. Follow the procedure for invoking the Divine Reiki Light (DRL). Close the eyes so that you can focus on the sensations better.
2. Intend that Mother Earth, the size and shape of an orange is floating in space . . . the colours are dull and not so clear, but as the DRL covers the planet and begins to heal it, this changes. . . .
3. Hold up the hands and also invoke the Opening Attitude of Gratitude for Mother Earth to open the hand channels for healing as well. (*'Reiki, please make Mother Earth healed whole and complete, so it is, thank you, Thy Will be done . . .'*).
4. Keep your elbows free, without resting them on anything; be aware of the feedback within yourself.
5. Intend that the following takes place as you are hearing this:

- The air of the planet is becoming clear and pure. . .
- The water everywhere is bright and sparkling fresh . . .
- All the plant-life and forests re-generate and cover the planet thickly . . . . Many valuable plants and herbs appear in order to benefit mankind.
- The animals, fish, birds, insects, bees, butterflies all live in abundance, receiving their share of resources from the planet so that they also peacefully evolve to their next higher level.
- The people of all nations are less tense and less anxious . . . see them smiling, relaxing . . . .
- The planet is being looked after and cared for by the people who live on it . . . all the natural resources of the planet are available in abundance . . . pollution and negative energies have dissolved, healed . . . .
- Your country is full of abundance . . all the people are happy, prosperous, joyous . . . see your city prospering beautifully, see your neighbourhood, your home . . . peaceful, clean . . . the people happy and satisfied . . .
- See yourself in your home with your family, the near and dear ones . . . if there are any issues you need to sort out with them, do so now . . . say and do whatever you need to in order to heal yourself and them . . . forgive yourself for your past . . . let go of it and see all the issues resolved as you express your love for them and also receive their love . . . loving yourself as well . . . .
- If there are any family members or dear ones who are no longer on this planet in their bodily form,

recall them as you last remember them, or by their names . . . say to them whatever . . . do whatever you need to . . . to heal your relationship and to complete with them whatever is unfinished still . . . experience this now . . . . See yourself and them . . . all healed and whole . . . .

- As the healing energies flow through you to them more and more, you too receive the healing more and more . . . becoming full with this . . . healed . . . happy, satisfied . . . . Forgive yourself for your past . . . for whatever wrongs you may have done . . . allow the Divine Reiki Light to wash over you—healing, soothing, loving yourself as you are, the way you are—unconditionally just as Reiki loves you unconditionally . . . .
- See your friends and others . . . faces known and unknown . . . all around . . . let them also be healed . . . see this happening now . . . as you see this, become aware of those who have not been so nice or good to you . . . who may have been actually damaging, harmful and even enemies . . . see them around you . . . as the unconditionally loving Divine Reiki Light heals them as well, you realize that something within you becomes lighter and lighter . . . follow this . . . letting go of blaming these others . . . experience how unburdened you feel when this letting go of pain and blaming takes place . . . experience this healing deeply now . . . .
- Allow your awareness to go to your work or your occupation . . . healing it . . . See your life as you would like it to be . . . successful, full of an abundance of health, wealth and joy . . . .
- See any life-situation problems that you might have . . . see this covered and transformed by the Divine

Reiki Light . . . harmonized, made well to your benefit . . . .

- And now see the whole of the country happy where no one lacks the basic needs for peaceful and a productive life . . . . Experience this . . . it expands to the whole world . . . the whole world is happy and healed and it is so . . . .
- As this happens, once again see the planet, Mother Earth, revolving in space . . . beautiful, beautiful colours, a rejuvenated world . . . with all the living beings on it healed, attaining their purpose in life . . . .
- Mentally declare: 'Mother Earth . . . and all those who appeared for this healing . . . are healed whole and complete . . . . So it is, thank you Reiki. . . . Thy Will be done. Thank myself, thank Mother Earth and all the healees who appeared in it . . . .
- With grateful thanks to the Divine Reiki Light—we request the Divine Reiki Light: *'Please be with Reiki, thank you!'*
- Lightly rub the palms of your hands together and gently draw them across your face. Open your eyes. This completes the healing.

*At the end of the first or first few such healings, you may feel:*

- Dizziness.
- Pain in the upper back and/or chest that ceases soon after the Mother Earth healing finishes. This is a very positive sign of the heart chakra opening up. (Persistent pain unrelated to this may need medical investigation.)

- Emotions coming up to the surface—wanting to cry. Allow this to take place. During this healing you have received a major healing yourself; something has dissolved allowing the emotions attached to float up to your consciousness while overcoming a physical block. This is the residue leaving—allow it to pass.
- Sweating, tingling, warmth and temporary aches and pains.

## DRL Applications Summarized

1. For settling issues, healing relationships, the healing may be done specifically for that purpose, intending in the DRL whatever you would like to see happening in order to have the issue resolved. *If you are not sure . . . just see/intend the end-result as being healed/ done in your favour.*
2. Healing many or one, the procedure is the same.
3. During the daytime or when you are in front of many people or travelling or driving, keeping your eyes open, the DRL may be invoked for an 'Instant Healing'. It is a simple practise.
4. Please note that this healing technique is not just positive thinking or imaging—it is empowered healing. A non-Reiki channel will get practically no results doing this. By the principle of energy following thought some benefit may be visible very, very slowly, but essentially this is a Reiki-empowered procedure for Reiki channels.
5. We highly recommend your sending healing to the whole world this way every day. As you do it, you will increase your healing capacity and also do a wonderful wide-ranging public service of the best sort.

You will be instrumental in removing and relieving pain from the hearts and lives of many. God bless you!

> You ask, 'How many people can I send healing to at a time?'. . . You can heal the whole world. First heal your inner world and automatically the outer is healed . . . and then when you work with sending healing externally you will see and realize that the whole world is healable. There is no limit to the number of people you can make healing available to with Reiki. It only depends on how much you can channel. The whole world needs a mega dose of healing—if you so desire to make it available then you also benefit. You receive 20 per cent of this mega-dose every time!

## Specific DRL Applications

### Examples

1. **Arguments/Disputes/Relationships (healing past events):** You may want to heal your relationship with your boss or others after arguments/disputes. Follow the procedure as described, replaying the situation in your mind, seeing/intending yourself and the other persons there and saying whatever you need to and doing whatever you need to in order to heal this.

   If you need to mentally get angry/violent while invoking the Divine Reiki Light—allow this to happen without feeling guilty—it will not harm you or the other person. In fact, if you have done the procedure properly and have a genuine Reiki connection you will not feel any anger shortly—whatever negativities and emotions you may be feeling slowly start dissipating and dissolving, lea-ving you peaceful and relaxed. This is contrary to what happens when we give vent to our anger—we start feeling more and more angry. With the DRL the opposite takes place.

Additionally, the persons will get the message, and when sufficient healing has been done, the situation gets resolved and healed as though nothing had been wrong in the first place.

2. **Healing those who have not asked for healing:** This can be easily done by *your* specifying an energy exchange! You can send healing to all the beggars at the traffic lights in this way sufficiently in advance, and through your whole journey, specifying: 'All the beggars at the traffic lights on my journey please take this DRL and in exchange do not approach my car, but find that car which will give you some donation, thank you.' This works as long as you do not start feeling sympathy or 'sorry' for them. The 'sympathy energy' will draw them to you regardless of the DRL.

   Similarly, when you send healing for a specific personal purpose, many people benefit. For example, you may Reiki through the DRL that, '. . . all the traffic lights on my journey to (specify the place) are green, with the traffic moving very smoothly and safely, and I have safely reached the destination.' Here all the drivers on the road, their passengers, the people on the streets, near the traffic light cross-ings will all receive healing. Continue the DRL until you reach your destination.

Another example: A college girl was being troubled by a boy's unwanted attention and she was advised by Renoo to Reiki him that, '. . . (boy's name) has found a better and more suitable girl and is no longer interested in (herself—name) . . . so it is, thank you, Thy Will be done.' The girl was surprised—('better than *me?*'—'*Yes!* Otherwise how else will he leave you alone? Do him and the other girl a good turn!') The desired result appeared in three days.

3. **Heal the future:** Intend the future event/situation and persons concerned are healed, the events having taken place as you would like them to.
4. **Heal the dead:** Intend that the absent persons are there in the DRL as you last recall them (or even if you do not know what they look like, intend they are there) and desire that they are healed, wherever they are. A particularly good time of the year to do this is during the *shraadh* period, although any time is a good time.

What is the need to heal the dead? Although the beings have changed their bodies, we may still have unfinished karmic business with them. Normally this means being re-born and paying off or receiving and collecting from them according to the unfinished account. Effectively, this means being tied up once again in the cycle of birth-death-rebirth—paying off karmic debts—receiving karmic credits from others and so on, endlessly.

As we have seen, only the divine can finish this—Divine Reiki. And this is one way. Whenever you get a persistent thought, idea—remember, it has appeared in your consciousness to receive healing. Send healing to the person, the situation. This is divine guidance or 'feedback' if you prefer.

5. **Protection:** Although you are at all times under special Divine protection once you are Reiki channels, if you are at any time worried or anxious that you are insufficently protected, ask for the DRL, intend that it comes out of your heart chakra and covers you on all sides, above and below in a beautiful blanket of love and light.

   This is especially powerful and useful to do if you are worried that you 'might catch some disease' by giving healing to someone. Please understand that while you are giving Reiki to someone, you **cannot** catch their disease. Reiki is a one-way flow only—it flows outward only. Nothing negative can come back to you, particularly as the principle of like attracts like will not allow negative energy to con-nect with the pure Reiki energy flowing from your heart (either through your hands while giving touch healing or directly from your heart chakra with the DRL).

   The mechanism of 'catching' disease germs operates only from the solar plexus area (the third aura body), where energies of 'sympathy', 'pity', 'poor fellow', etc., come from. The DRL protects you from this. *(For additional protection, see* *'Protection Shield', p. 190.)*

   Please remember: Fear and doubt are the greatest of disease attractors. Reiki your thighs and knees and root chakra sufficiently to counter this.

## REVIEW NOTES

**You can safely say and do whatever you need to in the Divine Reiki Light (DRL) to anyone in order to heal yourself or the situation.**

- If using only the DRL method (excluding steps 4.1 through 4.2, p. 181), no Opening Attitude of Gratitude is needed. (The Closing is needed.)
- After invoking the DRL, if you get distracted and involved in other work, 'forgetting' the healee—whenever you remember, declare the Closing for the healee, thanking the DRL. *This is not a 'mistake'*—the healee needed this healing time in the DRL.
- The DRL remains for six hours after invocation and will automatically disconnect from the healee after this time. In case you forgot to thank the DRL during this period, do thank the DRL when you remember, **declaring the healee to be healed.** (The Closing Attitude of Gratitude is needed, although the Opening is not required for the simple DRL method.)

# 28

# *The Protection Shield*

This protection prevents negative energies of others or the environment from contaminating our energy body. It prevents loss of our positive energies as well.

This shield is *essential* for daily use especially at offices, workplaces, marketplaces, crowded areas, parties and meetings, crematoriums, burial sites, restaurants, hotels, railway stations, airports, etc.

## Protection Shield Invocation

- The shield is constructed from purple coloured mirrors on the inside as well as the outside surfaces. This mirror surface is totally unbreakable by any known or unknown harmful thing.

- Imagine/*intend* yourself surrounded by two purple mirrored boxes, one close to you and the second box further away from you which is larger, and surrounding both you and the first box.

- The boxes have mirrors on the inside as well as the outside and have no openings. *The boxes can be as big as you want.*

## The Protection Shield

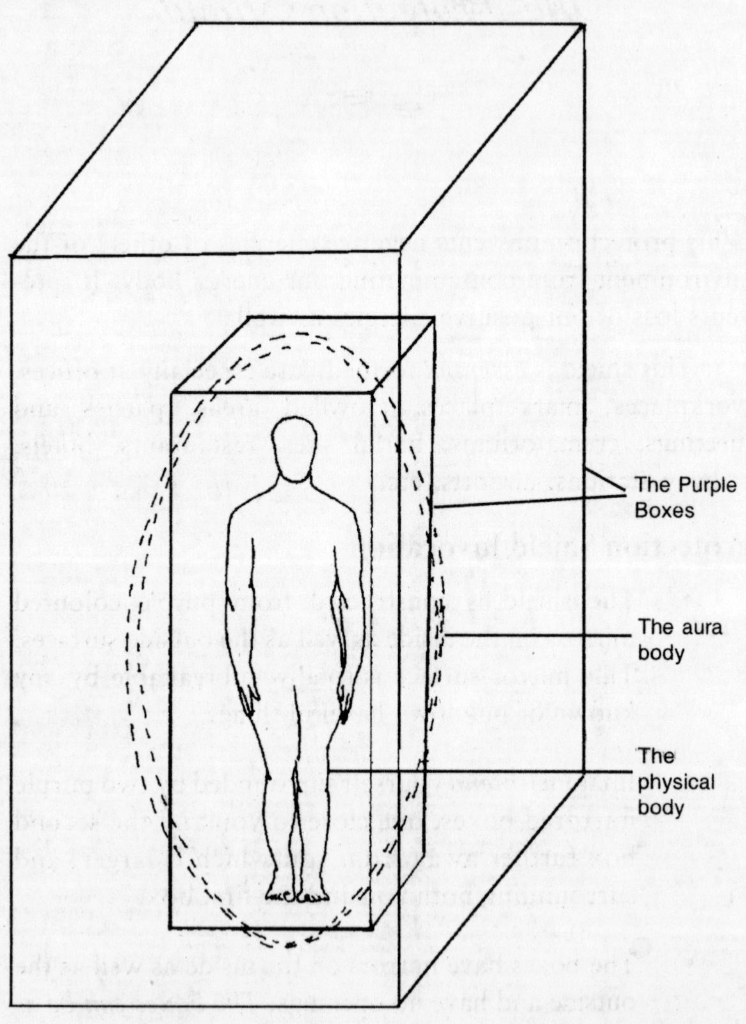

- Request the boxes: 'Please protect me and my aura invincibly against all human creation, allowing only love and light to pass in and out *as needed in my best interest*. Please give this protection from now until *(specified time)/(specified event)*. At which time please go back to the source as love and light—thank you . . . .'

CAUTION

- The shields should not be kept on for more than 12 to 14 hours at a time, and *never* while sleeping at night as it may lead to temporarily trapping more negative energies than can be transformed, creating uneasiness, bad dreams, etc.
- *Do not put more than one person in one protection shield. Each person to be protected must have them individual shield.* (*There is no shortage of shield availability*!)
- You may shield your home/office after it is energy clean (about 1 week of energy cleansing—See Appendix-3 'Energy Cleansing Measures for the Home and Workplace).'
- You may shield your car or motorcycle, bicycle or scooter, etc., immediately.
- *If at any time you start feeling uncomfortable/irritable* while having the shield protection on, send the shields back to the source as love and light and invoke a *new* set of shields. Or: invoke the violet flame for a short while.

## REVIEW NOTES

- The shield will be as strong as your intention and affirmation of safety.
- You can do Reiki, the DRL and the meditations while in your shields

# 29

# *Reiki Essentials Summarized*

- Reiki initiation or attunement is the process of opening a channel for cosmic healing and nourishing energy to flow. *Reiki* is 'Universal Life Force Energy', 'Unconditional Love Energy'.
- Initiation with Reiki affects each person differently depending on one's vibratory level. One can continue to increase one's energy level and healing capacity by treating oneself daily, and others whenever possible.
- The more healing you make available, the more healing you receive and greater 'positivities' are made available to you.
- Reiki healers are only channels for *making available* the healing energy—the healee heals himself by accepting this energy. Reiki channels are not doctors although some doctors may be Reiki channels. Reiki channels may not interfere with a healee's ongoing treatment—results, in time, show the potency of Reiki healing.
- Reiki is given on asking. It is *not* the job of any healer to help where healing is not wanted. *Even God does not enter where He is not invited. Do not throw Reiki.* 'Do not cast pearls before swine' (Jesus Christ). *(Exceptions have been indicated.)*
- There should be a mutual exchange of energies for the healer's time. Also, it is not right to keep a person indebted for services rendered. Be appropriate at all times.
- Do not be attached to results, but rather be *committed* to results by improving (healing) yourself and understanding how Reiki heals.

- To live in an attitude of gratitude is to experience a life full of abundance.
- Whenever a cleansing takes place, be thankful that the particular negativity is surfacing and request Reiki to send the emotion, and whatever it is attached to, back to the source as love and light.
- Do not pass judgements—instead deal with the situation, and heal it. *Reiki-1* is the first step towards becoming master of your destiny. This is not a small thing. You are no longer helpless in any situation anywhere, any time. *You can heal it now*!
- All negative emotions are attached to persons or events. One has to LET GO of the *whole package*. If 'blaming/holding responsible/judging' of the other is retained, the negativity of pain also stays, giving 'dis-ease'. 'Letting go = foregoing judgement = *Forgiveness*'. So, in your own self interest—let go!

### OFFENSE

The spiritual and Reiki *cannot* be overcome by any material condition, but may be *temporarily retarded* by OFFENSE against the spiritually elevated. The *root* offense is: Criticizing/judging Reiki channels and the spiritually elevated or *gossiping* about them. In Sanskrit this is known as *sadhu ninda—criticism against the correctly and purely placed.*

This *temporarily* blocks Reiki and can result in severe cleansing reactions. When you send 'not love' to someone in this way, by the principle of 'like attracts like', you also receive the same *at the level of the advancement of the spiritualist criticized.* If your 'digestion' is strong enough, then you can 'swallow' this. If not, then you receive reciprocal reaction as a life-situation (job/finance/relationship) problem or health problem. Abundance shrinks temporarily until you are cleansed of this offense.

# 30

# *The Five Principles of Reiki*

These are the most important guiding principles of living a life with Reiki, given by Dr Usui after deep meditation and realization. We have expanded these according to our realizations. If you remain aware of these principles in your daily life, you will find all guidance from them for every situation. (*Also refer to 'The History of Dr. Mikao Usui' in* **The Joy of Reiki** *written by the authors.*)

1. **Just for today, I will live in the Attitude of Gratitude.** Always feel thankful for what we have and whatever we need will be provided. Whatever we meditate on expands by the principles of 'like attracts like' and 'energy follows desires and thoughts'. With Reiki empowerment the effects are multiplied greatly and seen very quickly. Our normal 'healthy' state is all-sufficiency or abundance. Where 'dis-ease' is absent, abundance is automatically there. By living in gratitude one can positively shift one's existence internally and externally.

2. **Just for today, I will not fear or worry.** Worry, fear, anxiety, at its fundamental level, comes from an apprehension that 'I', 'my consciousness' will cease to exist. That I shall 'die'—cease to exist as I know it. Fear of 'what will happen tomorrow' or 'fear of the unknown' is the same fear—the fear of losing what I have today.

Even in this lifetime each of us has travelled in many different bodies, but our consciousness in terms of self-identity has remained the same always—whether five years old or fifty, the 'I' consciousness, the self-identity, remains the same although the body that was at five years old has long gone.

Modern medical science says that every seven years every single cell of our body has been replaced by a new one—so we do not even have the same cells we were born with. At the same time we are always aware that we are the same person, the same individual consciousness even though the body has changed radically.

Fundamental fear comes from being disconnected from the universal wholeness, the divine part of ourselves which is of the quality of Reiki love, eternal and deathless.

When you are connected fully with Reiki, the Divine, you will experience directly the qualities of the Divine including direct perception of your eternal higher self. This is self-realization and with it comes the perfect sure understanding that you are fully prot-ected through your connection with Reiki.

There is also a universal timing of events in life. Try not to interfere with it unduly but at the same time don't be helpless—in any situation you can always invoke Reiki intervention and harmonize it. Therefore, there is no need for anxiety. Live each day to the best of your ability with Reiki flowing through you and all else will be taken care of.

3. **Just for today, I will not anger.** Anger is a result of feeling out of control, helpless. 'I am the (supreme) controller or doer' consciousness is termed as *'ahankaar'* in Sanskrit. The equivalent translation in

English is: 'false ego' meaning 'false identification of self, of knowing who one is'. In Vedic terminology there is no word for false ego except *ahankaar*—I am the doer-controller.

This is false identification of self because we identify ourselves with the interaction of the material modes of nature—goodness, passion, ignorance *(sattva, rajas, tamas),* which are all changeable and perishable like the physical body. That non-permanent nature is also the cause of our feeling fearful, anxious, helpless, because we then naturally identify our essential self with non-permanence.

Only when we are fully connected with pure spiritual goodness *(shuddh sattva)*—pure *Reiki,* that we actually realize we are not the supreme controllers, and that we are also 'non-perishable'. That we too have the quality of immortality of consciousness, of being. And that consciousness has a form, a body in which to contain itself of a similar vibratory rate. Experience this yourself as you connect deeply with your essential self through *Reiki* empowerment.

As a Reiki channel, your awareness that you are a channel, an instrument for healing, dissolves the false identification. As you connect with your higher and perfectly pure self, your realization as to your pure spiritual identity is totally integrating. There is no controllership issue any more.

And until that happens, become aware of your reactions without judging yourself or trying to 'force a change'. Feel thankful for having an opportunity of becoming aware of a 'dis-ease' condition. Do not feel guilty for feeling anger: forgive yourself, *witness* anger. Let it go, and observe it dissolve in the act of witnessing it, becoming aware of it.

4. **Just for today I will do my work honestly.** Doing my work honestly today means not being burdened tomorrow by any lack in it which I may have prevented. Thus, there is no anxiety on this account. This also means correcting all that which prevents results, starting with *becoming aware of the blocks caused by my own attitudes and behaviour*—especially the action of the false ego: 'I am the doer.' If, having worked honestly, desired results are not there, it is Divine Will.

   At the same time I may not use this as an excuse to do my work casually—'I have done some healing work and now Reiki should do the rest. If the healing is not successful then that is Reiki's fault!' **Reiki is not my servant.** If the healing does not get the desired result then I must check where have I gone wrong—did I neglect something? Dr Usui found the beggars had no attitude of gratitude, they had not asked to be healed and there was no energy exchange: he rectified this. He did not say, 'Reiki didn't work!' because he fully realized the quality and potency of Reiki. Instead, he did whatever was required for getting the positive result.

   Therefore, a very major part of doing my work honestly is to understand how Reiki likes to work under different circumstances, and what I should do to get results.While not being attached to the results, not having a controller-doer identification, but the understanding that I am a channel, I am *committed* to the result. Neither casual, nor fanatic, not a 'life and death challenge' thing. Simply, steadfastly committed to healing my whole exist-ence *and whatever and whoever crosses my path.*

5. **Just for today, I will respect my parents, elders, teachers.** Respect means to give proper regard,

position, appreciation. Regardless of how good or bad our parents may have been to us, there is one thing that demands respect universally under all circumstances. Whether our parents were good to us, mistreated us, ruined our life, abandoned us or whatever.

The single reason universally applicable under all circumstances is that, *they gave us this bodily vehicle and shelter through which we can realize our life's goals and aspirations.* This is the only vehicle we have in this lifetime and whatever it is like, through it can be fulfilled all our life's aims. It gives shelter to our spirit, and without it we are not moving in *any* direction.

Why should we respect elders and teachers?

We respect them because their practical experience of life, and their knowledge imparted to us can speed us on in our daily business of life. We can profit from their experience, their practical wisdom, their teachings, which can earn us a respectable livelihood while avoiding unnecessary entanglements.

And spiritual teachers can impart *actual spiritual empowerment* and knowledge that removes ignorance and accompanying negative *karma,* and which at its highest levels puts us directly in touch with our pure spiritual self and the Divine.

Finally, accept *Reiki* as that teacher and your life will be sufficiently and perfectly healed, whole and complete.

Therefore, just for today respect parents, teachers, elders and *Reiki.* And when you see that all living beings have a *Reiki* connection, and the Divine is within them equally, there will be respect for all, automatically. Then your daily greeting to all will truly have meaning—*namaste:* 'I bow with respect to the Divine within you, to Whom my life is dedicated.'

And for now, be with Divine Reiki.

Flow with Reiki.

Just one day at a *time.*

NALIN NIRULA

RENOO NIRULA

> *This concludes the general, specific and confidential formal instruction at the First Reiki Initiation with Nalin Nirula and Renoo Nirula, Sensei.*
> *Reiki enlightenment makes you and your life whole and complete.*
> *And so it is.*

---

*Special Note:* The first principle of 'gratitude' is in fact a very sublime and highly developed one. In practise we find that for one to connect with this in actual fact is very difficult, especially as most people take this to mean a verbal or external show of gratitude. However, this is only partial and very incomplete.

We recommend that anyone who wishes to harmonize his life (whether a Reiki channel or not), should in fact *first* connect with the Fifth Principle of Reiki— 'Just for today I shall respect my parents, elders and teachers and all living beings (who have Reiki flowing in them—*including myself*).'

The respect principle means acknowledging that the other is superior to oneself in some way. (In one's own case it means respecting oneself and not judging-criticizing.) This creates a healthy space for developing harmonious 'non-threatening' interactions, not uselessly ruffling the false egos! By the universal energy principle of 'likes attract' the interaction or relationships become more stress-free. We once asked one of our spiritual master— 'Do we also have to respect someone who may be a rascal. And if so why?' And our spiritual master replied— 'Yes! Respect the fact that you can never be as superior a rascal as him! So respect even a snake!'

This is a *doing* principle, and similarly the Fourth Principle may be acted upon— 'Just for today I will do my work honestly.'

By these *action* principles we can gradually come to the point of internally and really being grateful and thankful, not artificially. Ultimately it is our actions and our inner condition that change things or impact on our lives and by working with these two principles we can get very good guidance on how to 'act rightly'.

# Appendices

# APPENDIX 1

## 'Instant Healing'

'Instant Healing' potential is available at every stage of your Reiki development. Any one or more of the techniques learnt and worked with thus far can be used as may be needed.

A typical full sequence of 'instant healing' may be as follows:

**REVIEW NOTES**

1. Invocation of Divine Reiki Light and or Reiki balls and sending to healee (do *not* specify any colour of the light).
2. Request Reiki to open/expand back heart chakra of healee.
3. Protection Shield for a specified time for the healee.
4. Temporary Chakra Balancing (Advanced Procedure in the Sealed Section at the end)

Finally: Your strong and genuine desire leads to healing . . . this is superior to all 'method'. Spontaneous healing takes place in the presence of a purified Reiki channel.

**'In an emergency, there are no rules or methods for healing—*it is just . . . done!'***

# APPENDIX 2

## The Self-cleansing Meditations

These meditations may be done by anyone (Reiki channel or not), for their benefit. These are very helpful in removing negativities from the body and organs and the aura. They may be done at any time for a few minutes each.

The meditations can be done indoors or outdoors. Doing these near or under a large tree is beneficial. *Do not do these while driving an automobile or operating machinery.* These are also available on audio tape and CD as the 'Joy of Reiki Meditations' with two additional meditations.

A good sequence is 'White Light' followed by the 'Violet Flame' and the 'Rooting'. Done before a bath, they are specially effective. (It is not essential to have a bath after these.)

They may also be done while you are in the Purple Boxes Protection Shield.

## The White Light Meditation (Gross Material Body Cleanser)

1. Intend that your body is a hollow cylinder. Focus on your breathing at the nostrils, being aware of the incoming and outgoing breaths.
2. Request Father-Mother of the Universe/God: 'Please send me cleansing beams of light at the palms of my hands and the soles of my feet, which beams send back

to the source all negativities as love and light, thank you.'

3. Request Father-Mother of the Universe/God: 'Please send me the White Light, thank you.'
4. Intend that a beautiful white light is descending from above, entering your crown chakra and filling up your hollow body. Allow the light to fill you up slowly inside and overflow outside.
5. Stay with this for a few minutes.
6. When you feel complete with this, thank the cleansing beams, the white light and Father-Mother God.
7. Request the cleansing beams and the White Light: 'Please go back to the source as love and light, thank you.'
8. Breathe deeply a few times, coming back to the consciousness of your surroundings. Slightly move your fingers and toes. Open your eyes.

*This concludes the White Light Meditation.*

## The Violet Flame Meditation (Aura Cleanser)

This Meditation may not be done when there is an open wound/recent surgery.

1. Focus on your breathing at the nostrils, being aware of the incoming and outgoing breaths.
2. Request: 'Saint Germaine, Keeper of the Violet Flame, please send me the Violet Flame to cleanse and purify me and the entire universe.'
3. Intend that a violet flame is appearing at the soles of your feet, entering the feet and body. The flame slowly travels upwards to fill you up from the feet to the top of the head and also covers you fully on the outside.

4. After a few moments, visualize and intend that the flame has expanded into a ball of about three metres diameter (9–10 feet) and that you are floating in the centre of this. Stay with this for a few minutes.
5. When you feel complete with this, thank Saint Germaine, the Keeper of the Violet Flame and the Violet Flame for cleansing and healing you and the entire universe.
6. Request the Violet Flame: 'Please go back to the source as love and light, thank you.'
7. Breathe deeply a few times, coming back to the consciousness of your surroundings. Slightly move your fingers and toes. Open your eyes.

*This concludes the Violet Flame Meditation.*

## The Rooting Meditation (Balancer, Anti-depression)

1. Focus on your breathing at the nostrils, being aware of the incoming and outgoing breaths. Visualize your body as a hollow cylinder.
2. Request Father-Mother/God: 'Please send me the White Light.'
3. Intend that a beautiful white light is descending from above, entering your crown chakra and filling up your hollow body. Allow the light to fill you up slowly inside and overflow outside.
4. Intend that *roots* are coming out from your root chakra and the soles of your feet. These roots are filled with the white light and go down to penetrate the earth below you. If you are seated and in a building, intend that the roots are penetrating your seat, the floor below, the space below and the next floor below and so on until reaching the ground floor. Then intend that the roots have penetrated the foun-

dation of the building, the soil, rock, under-ground streams of water, underground caves and more earth.

5. Request the White Light in your roots to heal Mother Earth which normally does not receive this light in this manner. Wait a few moments.

   Request Mother Earth: 'Please heal all the elements in my aura and physical bodies, thank you . . . . please heal the earth element, the water element, the fire element . . . . the air element and the space element and all their qualities. Thank you.'

6. Thank Mother Earth for healing you. Thank the White Light and Father-Mother/God for healing Mother Earth and you. Leaving the roots to find their stable depth, ask the White Light to go back to the source as love and light. Breathe deeply a few times, coming back to the consciousness of your surroundings. Slightly move your fingers and toes. Rub the palms of your hands together and lightly draw them across your face. Open your eyes.

*This concludes the Rooting Meditation.*

### MEDITATION NOTES

1. NO 'picturization' or visualization is required at all for any of the meditations. Just a simple mental *statement or intention* that 'such-and-such is taking place' is sufficient.
2. After making the mental statement for the meditations you can be engaged in doing other things for a few minutes—*no concentration is needed!*

### CAUTION

The Rooting Meditation may not be done in a moving vehicle, or aeroplane in flight.

# APPENDIX 3

## Cleansing Measures for the Home and Work Environment

These measures are very powerful for creating a positive energy field whereby the positive effects of healing are multiplied, and the measures themselves are cleansing and healing.

1. After doing the Violet Flame meditation for yourself, request the flame to leave your body and circulate around the home room by room, cleansing and purifying the areas—mentally intend the flame is going from room to room for a few seconds each. At the end of this, thank the flame, the keeper and St Germaine, and request the flame to please go back to the source as love and light. *(Do not get the flame back on your body!)* The flame is a cold fire, and will not appear on water. *Avoid circulating it near flammable material.*

   You may do this at your workplace, in hotel rooms, in public transport, in public enclosed places such as restaurants, theatres, etc., so that your space is relatively clean.

2. Evaporate **pure camphor crystals** on an electric bulb as on a table lamp. Alternatively, and most effectively, you may use an electronic anti-mosquito device and place the camphor on a used repellant mat or directly

on the metal plate, and this way the camphor evaporates slowly over many hours.

This purifies the area rapidly and is very healing. Special ceramic rings are also available which fit over electric bulbs and in which you can place pure esse-ntial oils such as sandalwood, frankincense, myrrh, juniper, pine, camphor, etc. These evaporate slowly due to the heat of the bulb.

3. Keep a bowl of **concentrated sea-salt water** in a corner of the living room or bedroom. This absorbs and destroys negative energy. Every few days put the bowl out in the sun for a few hours, add water if the water level has dropped due to evaporation. This is not needed if floors are mopped daily with water that has a handful of sea-salt added to it (10–15 litres of water).

4. **Fresh cut flowers with leaves intact**, placed in water, and **indoor plants**, are great positive energy generators and negative energy transmuters. Marigolds *(gainda)*, daisies and violets are most powerful for this.

5. Various **healing music** tapes are available and these are good for the energy body. Flute music is very good for healing the energy body. The music of Kitaro and Yanni is excellent for healing/meditations, as is the music of Pandit Hariprasad Chaurasia and Pandit Shiv Kumar Sharma.

# APPENDIX 4

## The Circle of Light

1. Two or more Reiki channels can increase and accelerate Reiki healing flow through the Circle of Light.
2. Stand or sit (without crossing legs/feet in the lotus position or *sukhaasan* position, or alternatively with legs stretched out in front of you) in a circle close to each other with fingers of the hands together, the hands slightly cupped.
3. Hold the left hand facing upward (receiving), the right hand facing downwards (giving).
4. Join the hands with your neighbouring channel—the channel on your left places his/her right hand over your left hand—fingertips contacting your finger-tips, the base of his palm touching the base of your palm; his right over your left. Similarly you place your right hand over the channel on your right side—your fingertips touching his/her fingertips, base of palm touching his/her palm.
5. A chosen group leader can direct the activities and call out the invocations: '*First, invoke the Divine Reiki Light and project it outward into the Circle.*'
6. Next, invoke: 'I thank myself for being here, I thank Reiki for being here, I thank the Circle of Light for being here. Reiki, please make the Circle of Light and all the healees that appear in it healed

whole and complete, So it is, thank you, Thy Will be done. . . .'

7. The individuals in the Circle of Light can start speaking the names of the healees (a person, a situation, a business, an activity, etc.) to be healed in anti-clockwise manner from the group leader's right. OR: simultaneously speak out the names of the healee person, situation, etc.

8. When everyone has named the healees, the group leader may say . . . 'Please intend and desire from your hearts that all the healees are receiving and accepting sufficient healing in order to be healed . . . with all negativities and cleansing reactions having taken place outside the aura of the healees and the Circle of Light and having gone back to the source as love and light (pause for as long as it feels right. . . one minute to a few minutes). . . .'

9. All declare after the group leader: 'All the healees are healed. . . '; 'So it is . . .'; 'Thank you . . . Thy Will be done.'

10.
   - 'We declare the Circle of Light to be healed whole and complete.'; 'So it is', 'thank you', 'Thy Will be done. . .'
   - 'We thank the Supreme Source of Reiki, Reiki and the Grandmasters and Masters of Reiki. . .
   - 'We thank the Divine Reiki Light and all the healers and healing energies . . . We request the Divine Reiki Light to please be with Reiki. . . . Thank you.'
   - 'We thank all the healees that appeared, we thank ourselves, and this opportunity for channelling healing. . . . Thank you.'

# SEALED SECTION REVIEW—ADVANCED PROCEDURES AND CONDITIONS—REIKI-1

*Please do not open the following sealed pages unless you have read and understood information on these pages. Thank you.*

Please study the advanced information in this sealed section only *after* you have worked adequately with all other procedures detailed in the earlier part of the book. This may be over a period from 7 to 14 days or longer.

*Give touch-body healing to others at least 15 times in order to get experience and understand feedback, etc., adequately before proceeding to the advanced review.*

Studying the *advanced* procedures without practical experience and working knowledge of the earlier detailed methods is of little use, because what is contained here is based on those earlier detailed methods and *without adequate practise you may be disappointed when results do not manifest.*

If you are ready for this next step, it means you have worked with the earlier detailed methods sufficiently and this will have given you a very respectable and respectworthy capacity for healing.

*You are to be congratulated on achieving this!*

*If, on the other hand*, you are not confident of these

techniques within a reasonable time of working with the methods given, then you need to spend more time healing yourself, especially at the root chakra and lower chakras (thighs, knees, calves, feet), and the back chakras.

The back chakras are relatively more important than the front ones as they are the 'input' or 'driving' chakras (the front are the 'output' chakras). There is a tendency to neglect these as sometimes (especially in the beginning of our practise) we may find the back positions 'inconvenient'. If such is the case, please rectify this and you will note a significant health benefit and life-situation benefit.

## 'I am not getting better/Reiki didn't work'

Please understand that as you affirm and think, so do events manifest. If you are stating regularly something to the effect that, 'I did the healing and the condition/the healing/didn't work . . . or . . . I didn't get well,' then that is what will manifest.

It may be that you are not aware of the benefits of the healing right now, but if you affirm the negative, it usually appears because you are a Reiki channel and your statements and words are empowered.

This is a demonstrable fact and you may be demonstrating it! So, better to say, 'every day, in every way, I am getting better and better,' rather than stating, 'I am not well'—*of course* you may not be well, and which may be the reason you did Reiki. This has perhaps been the settled condition and your negative affirmations about it do not help make you better. They retard healing because they become *self-fulfilling prophecies*!

When we find a block in our healing process, understand that the reasons are always internal rather than external, *provided you have received an authentic Reiki connection in the first place.* If you have done your homework well before applying for the Reiki attunement, then you should be at a good place with your Master. The key to finding a good Reiki Master is:

1. You yourself must be sincere in your desire to receive the highest and best *without* shortcuts!
2. All limited and conditional forms of Reiki such as Karuna Reiki, New Age Reiki, 'Om' Reiki, etc., do not produce the effects that pure traditional Reiki has. Such hybrid forms of Reiki may be avoided if you want to progress on a perfect path. At the same time, we see that many people will take to these lower, conditional forms of Reiki due to their karmic pattern and their inner development at that time.

   This is not a loss provided they understand that they need to progress further and seek out a Reiki Master from the pure traditional line who is practising traditional Reiki, not just claiming it to be so. Detailed information on this are available in our book *The Joy of Reiki,* Chapter 13.
3. If you have a genuine Reiki connection, but there is a problem of lack of knowledge or information, this book will rectify it provided you sincerely follow the guidelines and avoid the offense of criticizing Reiki channels or Masters.

We get the Reiki connection according to our own karma and inner attitudes. If we are looking for cheating shortcuts or 'easy' and lazy ways of achieving results, we invite being cheated. If you experience any blocks in the way of your healing, please go back to meditate on the fundamentals of Reiki—the Attitude of Gratitude and the rest of the Five Principles of Reiki.

## Feedback—A Further Understanding

After having done sufficient Reiki on yourself over a period of time, you will find that you are generally getting less and less feedback in terms of warmth/tingling, etc., when doing self-healing, although on receiving healing a healee may remark that your hands are hot. This is a good sign and means that there is less and less resistance to energy flow through your own channels which are now quite clear and open.

When feedback tells you that enough healing has been received at a particular point or place, it really means that no more energy is absorbable/required at this time. In other words, this particular health layer is 'full' and the 'ceiling' of the next layer is blocking healing. This is a 'block' which has to be penetrated in order for the healing to progress further. (Blocks can be dissolved using the Cleansing Beams at the back of the hands, as detailed in the section 'Doing Reiki Healing—General Guidelines', pp. 105–114.)

Schematically it may be useful to think of the healing process as a 'peeling off' process, such as peeling off layers of an onion. As each layer is removed (healed) another layer appears to receive healing. As the healing process continues, the areas being healed are moving more and more from the gross physical into the subtle emotional-mental.

## No Feedback

Sometimes you may have a condition where there is no feedback to tell you if energy is flowing. This may happen even though while giving healing, the healee feels 'heat/tingling' as a direct symptom of the Reiki flow. The reason for this is that the chakras of the hands are not sufficiently aligned in the various layers of the energy field and, therefore, you are not receiving the feedback although the energy is flowing as per feedback from the healee.

In such a case, always work confidently and with the understanding that Reiki is flowing. Sending a few minutes of healing daily or often to Mother Earth as per the procedure ('Heal the World') detailed earlier in the book will help to open your blocked channels in a big way and increase your healing capacity while also aligning your chakras.

## Cleansing

During all of this there may be periods of emotional cleansing coming up from time to time. Please avoid reacting or responding to situations as from a conclusive state—this is because whatever you may be feeling during this time is a condition in transition only—soon to evaporate leaving behind nothing. Therefore, avoid 'reacting', and understand it to be an old emotion attached to some person or event that is coming up in your consciousness or life on its way out, never to return again—provided you allow it to go. So let it go!

> Based on a review of the above, and an assessment of your present state of development, if you are now ready for working with the next steps of Reiki healing, *break the seal* on the following pages and study the information and practise the methods given sincerely. All success to you.

# Sealed Section
# (Advanced Review Notes)

# ADVANCED REVIEW NOTES

## Temporary Chakra Balancing

This procedure is very effective as an 'instant healing' component or a mini-healing. *Balancing chakras calms, soothes and harmonizes a person emotionally and mentally.* We have discussed earlier that 'energy follows thought' and impinges on people getting a similar response from them.

We also indicated that any negative thought or speech ought to be 'recalled and cancelled' (see the section on 'Intentions and Affirmations'.) Your thinking and speech as a Reiki channel is very powerful with Reiki behind it.

You can now mentally balance a healee's chakras in the following way:

Bring your awareness to your third eye chakra (focus your attention mentally there), and from there mentally address the healee's third eye chakra (inserting healee's name if known), *very gently:*

'(Healee's name's/this person in front of me, etc.) third eye chakra, kindly balance and harmonize *all* (healee's name's) chakras and systems in (healee's name's) bodies—thank you.'

For balancing a group of persons you can gently state:

'All third eye chakras present in this room/(at this traffic crossing/in this building/in a fifty metre radius) kindly balance and harmonize all your respective chakras and systems in your respective bodies—thank you.'

For balancing at a distance (Absentee balancing):

- Invoke the Divine Reiki Light (DRL) as per the procedure taught earlier.
- Intend the healee/s are in the DRL.
- Make the balancing statement.
- Thank the DRL and ask it to be with Reiki.
- No Attitude of Gratitude Opening/Closing is needed.

It is a simple mental request to the third eye (ajna) chakra from your third eye chakra with the force of Reiki behind it. ***Do not make a forceful request!*** If the result is not visible within two minutes, *gently* repeat the mental request and use additional methods as given below.

This procedure is very useful for dealing with an angry person or an emotionally upset/disturbed person. The result is usually there in 90 seconds. Combine this with the Purple Boxes Shield, DRL, Reiki balls/requesting Reiki to open the person's back heart chakra, and the results are there within 30 seconds—as long as it takes to invoke the procedures. *You can balance your own chakras this way once a day or more often if needed.*

## REVIEW NOTES

### Shields (Purple Boxes)
### Additional Utilities

The Purple Boxes Shields can be used for purposes other than protection.

Some of you may have observed or noticed that when the Purple Boxes are cancelled or leave after their alloted time, you may feel a little cold.

The reason for this cold sensation is that when the boxes leave, they take away the negative energy from the aura, and this 'evaporation' of negative energy creates a sensation of coolness. This may remain for a while if there is a time lag before the positive Reiki energy comes to fill the aura in its place.

We use this capability of the Purple Boxes to remove negative energy in a rapid manner from the total aura without touching the person. Thus, we may do this by invoking the Purple Boxes Shield for a few minutes at a time, and repeating this as often as necessary. There are four types of negative energy we can remove: (1) Sorrow/depression/guilt and self-blame/envy, hatred, etc.; (2) Pain and Fear; (3) Negative thoughts/obsessions; and (4) Negative thought entities.

### (1) Removing negative energy of depression/sorrow/ guilt and self-blame/envy, hatred, etc.

For example, someone is lamenting, crying about some emotionally painful/disturbing matter—invoke the Shield over them for three minutes, pre-programming that the Shields go back to the source as love and light after three minutes. You may do this a couple of times and you will find the person becoming calmer, more relaxed and much less stressed. Then invoke another Shield for a longer period, and use other distance healing methods such as DRL, Chakra balancing (which can be done once on first seeing the person).

Depression is coming from the hara and liver, so these areas may also be separately shielded for a short time (a few minutes) at a time and then sent back to the source as love and light.

## (2) Removing/isolating pain and fear

Pain and fear can be healed by first isolating it in a set of Purple Box Shields, and then sending healing through the DRL, etc.

For example, if someone has injured himself on the arm and is in pain:

- Shield the person.
- Shield the injured part by invoking a separate set of Shields for its (for, say, four hours).
- Shield the knees (for, say, one hour—'. . . protect the knees invincibly against all human creation, allowing only love and light as may be needed in (healee's name(s)) best interest for one hour at the end of which please go back to the source as love and light—thank you.').
- Shield the pain for 2-3 minutes ('Kindly protect Pain etc . . . .') requesting that the pain be isolated from the person—sending it back to the source as love and light along with the Shield. Repeat as often as neccessary until the pain the is relieved. Also use other methods as taught.
- Shield the solar plexus (for, say, one hour—invoking similarly as above).
- *Mentally balance the person's chakras.*

- *Send the Divine Reiki Light (DRL) healing.*
- Give touch healing at back heart and at/above injury site if possible.

## (3) Removing negative thoughts/obsessions

Mentally intend that the healee's negative thoughts or obsession is shielded for some time two or three times a day for short periods. For example: '. . . kindly protect (healee's name's) obsessive thoughts/negative thinking against all human creation, allowing only love and light in and out in the best interest of (healee's name) until (time by the clock) at which time [or (next xx minutes/hours), at the end of which time], please go back to the source as love and light . . . thank you.'

Doing this regularly has a remarkably healing effect.

## (4) Removing negative thought entities

Negative thought entities such as encountered in schizophrenia or multiple personality disorder can be healed in this way, along with using all other Reiki methods.

A negative thought entity can be isolated by your mental intention—intending and programming that the purple mirrored boxes are protecting 'the negative thought entities and their aura invincibly against all human creation, allowing only love and light in and out, in the best interest of (healee's name) until . . . (time) . . . etc., etc. (as above).'

Please remember—while the purple mirrored boxes shield is very effective for all these areas described, schizophrenia and multiple personality disorders are not a simple or easy disease to reverse. A lot of healing over a longer period of time is usually required.

Reiki-2s can use this and all other techniques taught with the additional empowerment of the mystic and sacred symbols of Reiki-2.

# LIVING THE FIVE PRINCIPLES OF REIKI—A PROGRESSED UNDERSTANDING

The spiritual essence within ourselves is always pure and does not need healing. The matter surrounding it needs to be healed in order to permit the spirit-self to shine forth. All spiritual efforts mean cleansing of that matter and the personal identification with conditioned matter.

That identification of self is the first and last obstacle in our own healing. This identification takes the false-ego platform, 'I am the doer'. In Sanskrit, this is termed as '*ahankaar*'.

Reiki is a beautiful spiritual connection that purifies us. During our cleansing process and looking for higher guidance much dust is thrown up. Often what we think is higher guidance is in fact deadly *ahankaar*. The antidote is Reiki and humility. The dictionary meaning of humility is simply: 'to be aware of one's own faults and defects'. Spiritual connection—the Reiki connection, awareness and subsequent rectification in fact and deed is the antidote to the victimization of matter.

Living the five principles of Reiki protects us from all material evils. We share our realizations on these with you:

1. 'Just for today I shall live the Attitude of Gratitude': All that comes to me comes from the Divine. Reiki channels are invited, called and summoned by the Divine for a higher purpose.

For being chosen as one who is being healed, through whom healing passes, and who is experiencing unconditional love of Reiki—this makes me naturally thankful and grateful. The more I convey healing, the more thankful I am.

Let me heal myself further so that I am able to convey even more healing. Soon I experience that the more healing I do outwardly, the more I am healed inwardly, and the more I heal myself by touch, the more the external world is healed. The Divine sends others to me for receiving Reiki's love and I must permit it to flow even to my so-called enemy. No holding back. This is possible only with empowerment through Reiki. As a natural unforced consequence I experience more Divine love, and hence gratitude.

2. 'Just for today I shall not fear or worry': Worry, fear arises first from fear of losing what I am att-ached to, and finally, from the ownership identification with matter. As I begin being detached, being a witness without accepting or rejecting, something different happens. Ownership-anxiety begins to dissolve.

   In practise, when I experience being a channel for the Divine, I realize the truth of 'like attracts like'—where I experience that the immortal, pure, joyous Divine touches and connects with me through that part of me which is also immortal, pure, joyous. I also see that Reiki looks after me, the Divine looks after me in all circumstances.

   I am not the doer, so why shall I worry?

3. 'Just for today I will not get angry': Anger arises out of a lack of control of the situation facing us internally and externally. We are unable to be the controller-doer and this angers us, depletes us, contaminates us. Reiki

and the Divine are the doers. Reiki channels are just that—channels.

The external world is only a mirror of our internal condition. If I see something that angers me, I should see that the anger's source is within and not outside. My internal condition is what I can and must deal with and resolve, and the external will soon come to reflect this. If enough of us do it, the world is healed visibly, very significantly.

I shall not anger.

4. 'Just for today I will do my work honestly': If I am not the doer, it does not mean that I shall do nothing. I must do my work honestly and completely and leave the results to Reiki and the Dïvine. I shall not be lazy, expecting Reiki to heal someone, and that is enough, having pushed the responsibility onto someone else.

   I must invoke healing with compassion, gentleness, care and commitment but not attached to the results. Therefore, I must constantly work at understanding how Reiki functions under different conditions. I must be connected and aware. The one closest at hand is myself, so let me heal myself and learn from the shades of my experience the certain knowledge that arises out of realization that the mechanism of the other person's illness is no different from mine. We are each similar to the other.

5. 'Just for today I will respect my parents, elders, and teachers': The dictionary explains 'respect' as a 'feeling of liking, approval, having regard for someone—to give everything its proper place, position'. When we can respect our parents, elders and teachers we can connect sincerely with others. All beings are connected to the Divine through Reiki. Reiki, unconditional love flows within them as well as it flows through me. That flow of spiritual connection links us and draws my automatic

respect, my regard. Those that are Reiki channels or spiritually elevated attract a special esteem.

In a hospital of sick people some doctors are there, and the rest are the sick. On this planetary hospital we see sick people who are not really themselves. We were also sick, but now are less sick. And if we are not ourselves entirely, and they are not themselves, what judgement shall we pass on anyone? If someone has come for being healed he is naturally not in a good condition, otherwise he would not be here—just like us—and, he has been sent to us by the Divine. So what judgement shall we pass?

The most fallen person healed knows most sharply the contrast between his earlier condition and his experiencing of Reiki, unconditional love. He experiences the Divine within and shows signs of the Divine's manifestations within him. We see the Divine within all beings—covered up perhaps, but very much there. So what judgement shall we pass where the Divine is?

Criticizing or judging anyone from the false ego platform is a hindrance to our own spiritual development and conmnection with Reiki. For some temporary false illusion of being 'superior' we pass judgement. So, 'just for today I shall not pass judgement but respect all living beings.'

'Just for today' focuses me in the present, the now in which I act and live—not a theoretical tomorrow sometime in the never-appearing future. Today is where I am and must deal with things that present themselves at present! Let me live and move through life just for today, completing all that needs to be done. And so just for today I shall not anger, not worry, do my work honestly, respect all living beings and be in an attitude of gratitude.

The way of Reiki is a daily process.

# FINAL INSTRUCTION

Reiki is a natural spontaneous healing flow from the heart. Ultimately there is no technique, no method of healing—just the presence of a purified Reiki channel creates a healing atmosphere. Sometimes such healing will take place in your presence . . . this is a sign that you have accumulated much Reiki and it overflows to others.

How often do you need to Reiki for self-healing in such a condition?

*Every day.*

As Reiki Masters, we need to place our hands on different parts of the body and do our self-healing as well. This keeps us fit and the Reiki free-flowing in all our channels.

A good programme to follow to flow with Reiki 24 hours a day is:

- Wake up in the morning and at that time *Close* the Attitude of Gratitude. This makes a very powerful affirmation for you for the whole day as the accumulated overnight Reiki energy flows to make this come true.
- Do the cleansing meditations (even while in bed) for a few minutes each (White Light, Violet Flame, Rooting).
- Open the Attitude of Gratitude for yourself and start the healing again, doing some formal healing at

various points, and the rest during the day in parts as may be convenient.

- Keep the Reiki flowing ('on') throughout the day and whatever you physically touch will also receive Reiki.
- There is no 'excuse' for 'not having time' to do Reiki. This only means deep-rooted negativities are preventing you from progressing. *There is no need to be helpless* when you are a Reiki channel—ask Reiki to help you. Put such an affirmation in your Reiki Box: '(Your name) has enough time to do and complete his/her Reiki self-healing every day . . . so it is, thank you, Thy Will be done.'
- Be creative, but remain within the trend of the guidelines given. Avoid speculation.

—Reiki love and light guide you and be with you in all your journeys !

*—Nalin Nirula and Renoo Nirula*

# APPENDIX S1
# REIKI-1 SEMINAR FORMAT
# DAY ONE

The format given below is a typical format for our *Reiki Experience™ Seminars* with typical timings. These will naturally vary according to the material covered and time spent answering questions and the size of the group. *The Living Handbook of Reiki* may be used as a standard manual of instruction and information.

At the initial stages, the Reiki Master may wish to have fewer participants, perhaps 6 to 12. He may then increase to a comfortable number where he may answer all questions and allow new concepts and the healing to filter through to the participants.

Group Reiki seminars are very valuable because when the group shares its experiences and joys and sorrows, all learn from it. It bonds them together and heals their inter-related group karma.

## Administrative Information

We announce the Reiki-1 timings as: 9:30 am sharp (9:15 preferable) to 6:30 pm and try and finish the first day's work before 6:00 pm, and remind people that the second day—'tomorrow may take longer depending on your questions and so on, so be prepared to stay a while longer.' *No cellular phones or pagers allowed*. (No smoking anywhere on the seminar premises—smokers are given opportunities to smoke outside the building.) The review meeting date and time is announced on the second day. The Reiki-1 certificates are handed out on the second day at the end of the seminar.

## Atmospheric Cleansing

During the seminar much negative energy is discharged. The area constantly needs subtle healing/cleansing. The minimum measures are: oil lamp and candles burning; constant steady evaporation of *pure medicinal camphor*; blowing of conch shell before participants arrive; having fresh cut flowers in water, indoor plants; cleansing the room with the Violet Flame periodically, sending healing to yourself and participants throughout the seminar, and in advance of it.

1. (About 09:30 am): *Register* participants, fill and hand out name tags.
2. (About 10:00 am, tea/coffee and cookies served): *Group Introduction* to each other—name, occupation/profession, and the reason each came to Reiki. (Some will not know, or say, 'curiosity'—in fact many may not know *why* they came!). They have developed sufficient positive karma so that they are able to come to Reiki—Reiki calls them. The Master introduces himself, giving background of how he came to Reiki.
3. (About 10:45 am): *Basic first two energy principles explained*—'Energy follows thought', and 'Like attracts like', (examples)—demonstrate and make group feel their own pranik energies and do the pranik energy ball generation and self-healing. Explain: This is subtle pranik (life-sustaining) energy from the individual's own limited aura or energy body as opposed to spiritual Reiki energy. *(Answer questions briefly.)* (After receiving the Reiki, energy balls made

from Reiki can be generated and sent—second day, experience the difference.)

04. (About 11:15 am): 10-minute toilet break—**no smoking** as attunements are to follow soon—smoking time shall be given after that.

05. (About 11:30 am): *Narrate the history of Reiki and Dr Usui.*

04. Speak and explain the *Attitude of Gratitude Opening.* Make all participants repeat their own Opening Attitude of Gratitude.

05. *Demonstrate the 31 point-positions*, explaining this as the **natural order of Reiki flow** and most efficient for healing: For the first 21 days it is desirable to do the self-healing in this order, especially so that one may not forget to do a particular position. In case one forgets, whenever remembered, do the position. If sometimes the order is changed but all positions are done—*there is no problem!*

06. (About 12:15 pm): *Commence attunements*, three or four persons at a time, each batch taking about 20 minutes. Meanwhile, participants may quietly pra-ctise doing their own self-healing positions with a music tape giving a gong/bell every three minutes to mark change of position. After people get attuned they may come back to the room where the others are and continue the self-healing without any discussions with each other.

07. (Before lunch, about 1:15-1:45 pm): *Briefly share experiences* each may have had during the attunements and thereafter (about 15 to 25 minutes depending on size of the group)—not for the purpose of comparison but only for the purpose of sharing varieties of experience that each may have had. If someone did not experience anything, it does not

matter—the work has already been done. The lower mind is sometimes very active preventing connection with the higher experience, and sometimes it does not remember what happened. *It does not matter because such experience is no indication of one's level of Reiki connection.*

Often people will cry or even vomit with the depth of emotions released after the attunement process—no sympathy or physical touching please, and do not allow any of the group to do the same—let the negative energy go. Touching the person at that stage with 'sympathy' or 'poor thing' energy will transfer the initiate's leaving negative energy to the person sympathizing.

07. (About 1:45 pm) Lunch break (smoking outside the premises only).

08. (After lunch, about 2:30 pm—Total time seven to eight minutes): *'Post-lunch Ayurveda'* (exercise to improve digestion very significantly): Make the participants lie down on their left side (with one leg drawn up comfortably if they so wish) for one minute, which is easily calculated by counting the in and out breaths. 16 in-out breathings at rest equal about one minute. When the participants are lying on the left side, the left nostril will block up and the breath will come from the right nostril (or sometimes both). Lying on the left side switches on the body's digestive system to 'high'—the breath coming from the right nostril is the 'sun channel', or fire. Fire exists in the body in the form of an oily liquid according to ayurveda. (Enzymes, bile and stomach acid.)

After one minute, turn to lie down on the right side for two minutes or 32 in-out breathing cycles. This switches the breath naturally to the left nostril—the 'moon channel' or cooling system, which prevents 'overheating' and consequent acidity and indigestion.

After this, turn to lie on the back with arms and hands in a relaxed position for four minutes or 64 breathing cycles. Knees may be drawn up if so desired. Then turn on the right side and come to the sitting position. Or—

09. (2:40 to about 2:50 pm): *Cleansing Meditations*: Continue from this lying-on-back position to the White Light and Violet Flame meditations. Speak out the meditation without any background music, taking about three minutes for each meditation. (These meditations are available on the 'Joy of Reiki Meditation' audio tape and CD—but avoid doing these during the seminar.)

    This is especially useful to give the participants the idea that they can invoke these meditations at any time and place. Explain that they can invoke these meditations at any time and place. Explain that they can now do it at any time anywhere with eyes open whenever they need to do so. (You may do the Rooting meditation also after this.) *Short Discussion.*

10. (About 3:10 pm): Cover the other *energy principles*—karma; what is right and wrong, what is the standard; what does blaming someone mean and consequent 'letting go' of blaming (forgiveness) is a major healing for oneself.

11. (About 4:00 pm): *Teach the Divine Reiki Light Method (DRL) of sending distance healing by first explaining* the basic procedure and then doing the Mother Earth healing—'Heal the World'. Discussion of sensations and feedback. (Pains in upper chest and mid-back = heart chakras opening—very good signs.) As much healing as we give, that much

we receive. Healing the world draws huge healing from us and opens our own channels more and more. (20 per cent is our share anyway!)

This method also details in short the type of uses we can make of the DRL such *as healing relationships, healing the dead, healing future activities, the business/work/events, etc. We recommend sending a few minutes of healing to the world every day.*

12. (About 4:45 pm) (Tea break: 15 minutes): *Review* any questions the participants may have without losing focus of main issues.
13. (About 5:00 pm) *Review the Attitude of Gratitude statement (opening)*, we normally teach the Closing the next day. Review all the 31point-positions. Explain that after finishing the self-healing, right hand on the heart chakra and left on the hara is very good for healing deep hurts, the past, the false ego, and for loving ourselves. *(The 'heart and hara' position)*
14. (About 6:00 pm) Caution participants: no discussion of the confidential material taught with non-Reiki channels, especially that of distance healing measures (DRL), etc., nor discussion of what they experienced during the attunements.
15. **Homework:** Full touch-body self-healing at all 31 point-positions. If any points are left to be done by the next morning, it can be completed it in the seminar hall when they come in next day.

    *Inform and Remind* healees that depending on questions asked, etc., and time taken for this, tomorrow they should be prepared to stay for a little longer period of time. (If questions get too far afield, ask them to keep these for the review session to be held 21 days later.)

**Note:** The Reiki self-healing may be done in parts and timed not according to the clock or the bell music, but by the feeling when each point has had enough Reiki. (One Reiki channel shared that he listens to Hindi pop music while doing Reiki, not because he likes the songs as much as the songs are usually three minutes in length and give him some idea of time without being stressed out!) However, if you can avoid it, avoid formally timing yourself, allowing the feedback mechanism to guide you.

Some days you may find a particular point-position needing more than three minutes of Reiki, on other days, somewhat less. Overall, adults may formally do 93 minutes (31-point positions × 3 minutes each) of Reiki, and while keeping Reiki 'on' during the rest of the day, whenever they have a few minutes they can do touch-body Reiki.

If the AOG is already on, no need to re-state it—but if the feeling comes, allow it to be expressed naturally. Be simple. Be in touch with your feelings, your inner self. This first day after attunements, full touch-body Reiki may be done in part the same day, balance the next morning. The next day full touch-body has to be done again to keep the continuity of the unbroken 21-day consecutive healing cycle.

Note : If the students appear not to have experienced any significant changes after attunements and cleansing meditations—get them to do touch-body healing on each other on the first day itself. Postpone the DRL and some of the theory/questions and answers to the second day.

*End of First Day*

# APPENDIX S2
# REIKI-1 SEMINAR FORMAT
# DAY TWO

01. (About 09:30 am): Participants to complete their Reiki, or do 'heart and hara' if finished with the full body. No discussions, no talking.
02. (About 10:00 am): Do the 'Joy of Reiki Meditation' from the audio tape/CD of the same name. Brief sharing of experiences. Follow up with the 'Sound of the universe' meditation on the same tape/CD. (Cleanse the room with violet flame and other cleansing measures).
03. (About 10:45 am): Simultaneous discussion and 15-minute tea break.
04. (About 12:30 pm): 'Higher Self meditation': (see para 8) Available on audio tape/as transcript for Reiki Masters—write to us.
06. (About 1:15 pm): Discussion.
07. (About 1:30-2:00 pm): Lunch
08. (About 2:15 pm): 'Post-lunch Ayurveda' followed by 'Higher self meditation' if not already done. Discussion.
09. (About 2:30-2:45 pm): Form partner groups and receive/give Reiki healing, Partial-point Reiki as there may not be enough time for full touch-body Reiki—45 minutes, demonstrate and have them do chakra balancing—15

minutes = 60 minutes each. Total time = about two hours if doing partner Reiki (two sets). (*If time is short:* have the participants do group healing: a number of healers simultaneously give healing to one person at different points.) If enough time is available for partner healing, do that and at the end inform them that if 'group healing' is given, the whole healing time taken is cut short.

10. (About 4:45 pm) (Tea): Discussion of feedback—heat/ no heat, etc.

11. (About 5:15 pm): Distribute *The Living Handbook of Reiki* and review the whole course broadly and very briefly, stating at each section of the book covering that topic, that the information has been covered, the participants can study it in detail—if there are any doubts or lack of clarity at that point, answer the questions precisely and briefly and patiently.

    A good way to do this is to go over the sections sequentially as they appear, stating, 'all this has been done already . . . the information is here if you need it.'

    *Hold at least one review meeting, say,* 21 days later (some of the participants will have had cleansings like clockwork on the seventh, eighth or ninth day). Deal with doubts, etc., at that time—inform the participants that this would be done.

    - Caution against sharing confidential information with non-Reiki channels or giving healees and others too much information.
    - Basic information on Reiki that may be shared freely as in the section 'Meaning and Features of Reiki'.
    - Review the universal energy law statements, and at 'Energy follows thought/Like attracts like' let all participants generate Reiki balls (by first mentally

requesting Reiki—'please generate Reiki healing balls please' or similar intent/request) and send to their own back heart chakra and feel the difference between the pranik ball generated yesterday and the Reiki energy today.

- Attitude of Gratitude (Opening) and (Closing) ('Already done') '. . . Energy Exchange'. . . .'Asking for healing . . . in practise what this means . . .'.
- 'Reiki Healing'—how it is done has been experienced, proceed through the section on the 31-point positions—noting that all drawings are given and there is no confusion of positions because by now all have sufficient practise—if there are any questions on this—quickly deal with it, refer them to the drawing or demonstrate the relevant position again.
- *Removing blocks* by calling Cleansing Beams.
- Review 'Offense', healing those who do not ask or want to be healed (non-acceptors).
- Review 'Emotions and the Body' and the 'Body Parts, Diseases, Emotions'.
- 'Repertory of Disease and Corresponding Chakras/ Points to Reiki' . . . review and remind that following one's feedback is very important as well.
- Go over sections: 'Self-healing', 'Giving Healing', 'Chakra Balancing', pointing these out, stating, 'all this has been done already . . . the information is here if you need it'.
- The 'Universal Emotional Energy Principles' are there in handy practical application form . . .'
- 'Intention Reiki . . . Distance healing through the Divine Reiki Light . . . Healing the World . . . all

these are here in sufficient detail . . .'

- 'The Protection Shield (Purple Boxes) . . . Reiki essentials is a progressed expansion of basic Reiki information . . . Affirmations, Intentions, Reiki Box healing—Why you must use Reiki in all things in life . . . (it cuts karma and karmic reactions) . . . Forgiveness—this may be shared with all—if one can let go, forgive, there may be no need to do anything else, love will flow!'
- 'Five Principles of Reiki and the Appendices may be studied . . .'
- '. . . And then there is a sealed section at the back: this may be opened only after you have done sufficient Reiki work and got some practical understanding of how energy works in health and disease—in 21 days or so (or to be opened at the Review meeting with the Reiki Master who would explain this further).'
- Demonstrate the Circle of Light. End—thank the Supreme Source of Reiki, Reiki, all the Grandmasters in the line by name, your Master and all genuine Reiki Masters in creation, thank those who guided or introduced each participant to Reiki; 'thank the seminar, all the energies and energetics that appeared in it, thank yourselves for accepting Reiki.'
- Distribute certificates and conclude.

Note: Depending on the individual requirements of each group, this order of instruction and topics covered would need to be adjusted. The emphasis or detailed instruction required for each group would also be different.

# APPENDIX S3
# REIKI-1 SEMINAR SIMPLE FORMAT FOR CHILDREN AND OTHERS

In our experience once the children receive their attunement, they become overactive and it becomes difficult to convey any further knowledge of procedures/techniques. In such cases (especially with younger children) we give the complete knowledge before attunement. With a very young group (8-10 years) we do not get to explaining the five principles until they have developed sufficiently with Reiki. We like to be in touch with all our students and guide them on an ongoing basis.

The simple format given below is useful for children (8-8½ years) upto and above the age of 14. We find this useful also for persons who may be very ill but want to help themselves. (Schizophrenic/multiple personality disorder conditions may first be given sufficient healing before attunement.)

The basic minimum format is:

- 'Like attracts like' and 'Energy follows thought' explanation.
- Generating pranik energy ball—experiment.
- Feeling emotions— 'indigestion' = being sick: (chain)
- Disease resulting in 'no flow' of Divine loving energy—restored by Reiki.

- What is Reiki, how it works (brief).
- The brief history of Dr Usui and Reiki.
- Arising from Dr Usui's history—two practical principles of healing—(i) healee must ask/want to be healed; and (ii) energy exchange; AND five principles (precepts) of Reiki . . . 'Just for today . . .'.
- Attitude of Gratitude explanation (AOG)—Opening.
- Listing of 31-point positions—demonstration.
- All state AOG (opening) for themselves.
- Attunement, while rest of group practises self-healing.
- Brief sharing of attunement and self-healing experience, feedback.
- Lunch.
- (Cleansing meditations—optional; and/or 15 minute-nap after lunch.)
- Younger children need not do full-body Reiki for more than 15 minutes per day. Teenagers may do for about half an hour a day, that is usually enough.
- Teach different ways of healing, and expand on them as per the capacity and interest of the group. (Reiki balls now rather than pranik balls; Reiki Box; Divine Reiki Light method.)
- Special healing methods for the life-situation problems of the group, for example the children's group will focus on schoolwork/homework, teacher and peer group problems; parent-children relationships, etc.
- Partner Reiki—practise giving healing to each other. Discuss feedback—21 days' self-healing and beyond . . . discuss.

- Shield protection (Purple Boxes).
- Circle of Light—Conclude.
- Distribute manuals and certificates.

The above programme may be comfortably completed from about 9:30 in the morning until about 5:00 pm with appropriate breaks in between for snacks, lunch, rest, tea-break—play outdoors for half an hour, etc.

Children are much less blocked than adults, and very quickly grasp the potential of Reiki and what they can do with it—no long proof/evidence chains are required for them. They sense things directly much more easily than adults and thus less time is required in getting them to understand the principles and applications of Reiki.